For Jan,

Me? A Caregiver?

A MEMOIR BY
MARY BETH HARRIS

*Thank you for
the reading list +
enthusiasm on
Africa! Heres to
more get togethers!
♡ Love
Mary Beth*

Illustrations by Janet Harris Bowe

Printed in the United States of America

First Printing, 2013

ISBN 978-0-615-70887-4

Incha Publishing
P.O. Box 253
Carmel, CA 93921
meacaregiver.com

Book design by Frank Chezem

For Mama

When you run into a friend whose loved one recently passed on, let them do the talking. This is not an appropriate moment to share your despondent experiences. This time is about them. Not you. Don't talk. Listen. Please remember this piece of advice.

ACKNOWLEDGMENTS

This book never would have been launched if certain friends and acquaintances hadn't offered to take my hand for a brief moment, walked with me and lent me their ear. Shortly after the conception, when the manuscript was quite rough and dreadful there were those who saw potential and encouraged me to continue. Marlene Martin, Nicki McMahon and Gita Caplan politely listened to re-write after re-write (even when I bored myself) and they urged me to keep going.

Thank you Jackie Fox, my brilliant friend, consultant, editor and diligent proofreader. Jackie articulated the parts that she enjoyed with enthusiasm and laughter and she very gently pointed out my errors and her concerns. I was pleased that she shared it with her highly qualified husband and also my dear friend Marty Veselich whose comments and opinions I deeply value. Thank you Marty.

My captivating friend, mentor, author and founder of Nightwriters writing seminars, Phyllis Theroux, reluctantly offered, "I will read only twenty pages and I will be brutal." Then two days later at her book signing at Harrison Library in Carmel, she spotted me and said, "I read the whole manuscript and liked it." Thank you Phyllis for the productive and pleasurable week I spent working with you in your charming writer's cottage in Ashland, VA.

My talented sister, Janet Harris Bowe showed her love and support by enthusiastically listening to each chapter then created the most amusing but candid illustrations. If you don't know me or didn't know Mama, I can assure you that Janet captured not only our physical likeness but she understood the spirit of our journey.

Shary Farr, Founder of Partners for Transitions, was unyielding that I finish this book. I can't imagine how Mama's life or my life during this time would have been without Shary and her never-ending love. Her kindness and compassion is unmeasured. Her knowledge and skills are invaluable. How do I thank an angel in street clothes?

My sister Susan's boundless support and persistence that I finish this book was the driving force to the end. She sat with me for hours listening to chapter after chapter then she stayed by my side as we proofread together. I'm not so certain that this book would have ever gone to print without her picking me up when I faltered and loving me so unconditionally from the moment I entered this world. My love and appreciation for my big sister is infinite and our bond is divine.

I am indebted to the extraordinary Carmel Foundation who delivered delicious dinners for a minimal fee when I lived with Mama. The Carmel Foundation then generously lent us a wheelchair, commode, and shower chair when Mama lived with me. The Carmel Foundation is a treasured asset to our community.

CONTENTS

INTRODUCTION

It was a huge production. A hospital bed and an airflow mattress were ordered. Mama's twenty prescriptions and eleven bottles of vitamins had been updated and transferred to a closer pharmacy. Caregivers lined up to be interviewed, hired, presented with a detailed job description, and trained. Visiting nurses and physical therapists prescribed by Dr. Hart needed directions.

I purchased diapers, wipes, under pads, tissues, and latex gloves discounted in mass quantities online. They were stacked all over the large room. I'd ordered an electric lift chair off the Internet but it was the wrong size, wrong color, and poorly constructed. It sat in its box labeled TO BE RETURNED, and on top of it sat new sippy cups, a huge bottle of baby powder, a tube of A & D diaper rash ointment, and a clock.

The temperature was high into the 90s as I sat on

a borrowed commode from our wonderful Carmel Foundation. A hospital tray (also borrowed) served as my desk, and it was piled high with papers and three days of unopened mail. A new mega-size box of Tylenol and a tall glass of iced tea sat at the edge. Sweat poured continuously down my brow and fogged the readers perched on the end of my nose. The oscillating fan didn't do much but send papers flying to the floor.

I glanced at the clock and noticed that the hospital bed should have been delivered over an hour ago. I would call them next, but first some of Mama's money needed to be transferred from one account to another and a prayer needed to be said that the money would hold out. As I waited for Mr. Logan (Mama's finance guy) to answer, I searched through the mess of papers for the Home Hospital Care number. I spotted it as Mr. Logan answered. He had handled Mama's finances for years, so the transaction went much smoother than tracking down the overdue hospital bed. I then dialed the Home Hospital Care number and the phone just rang and rang. I was about to hang up when someone answered.

"Hello, Home Hospital Care, Andy speaking. May I help you?"

"Hi, this is Beth Harris, is…" I scrambled for the contact's name on the small business card "…Margaret there?"

"Sorry she stepped out for lunch. Is there something I can help you with?"

"Well, I ordered a hospital bed which was to be delivered

today between 10:00 am and noon. It is now after 1:00, the bed's not here, and I am concerned."

"Let me see if I can help you with this. Can I put you on hold?"

Oh God! I remembered previously being put on hold at Home Hospital Care for what seemed like hours. First deafening music, then an announcer who sounded like a game show host. I wasn't at all up for that, but I had stuck a fresh estrogen patch on that morning and felt polite. "Sure, I'll wait."

Then I heard it. The loud ghastly music, then that voice. "HOME HOSPITAL CARE. WHEN YOU BRING A LOVED ONE HOME, BE PREPARED. WE SUPPLY OXYGEN, HOSPITAL BEDS..."

Luckily I heard Andy's voice back on the line. "Uh, ma'am? When was that order called in?"

I rolled my eyes towards heaven and thought, *Oh hell, here we go again. Stay calm.* "It was faxed to your office Tuesday for delivery today between 10:00 am and noon. I am concerned because I am picking up my disabled mother from the nursing home around 3:00 and I need to make up the bed. I need it here ASAP."

I heard Andy riffling through papers and I sensed his nervous energy. I picked up the cold glass of iced tea and held it against my sweaty forehead, then closed my eyes and took a deep breath.

"Uh, ma'am? Who was the doctor that prescribed the bed?"

I moved the glass to my chest. "Dr. Hart ordered the

bed on Tuesday. His nurse faxed the order to you around 10:00 that morning. Is there a problem?"

"I hope not ma'am. I..."

I was getting agitated every time I heard "ma'am." I had to interrupt. "Excuse me, Andy?" Another deep breath and I said to myself, *Remain calm, remain calm, and remain calm.* I exhaled. "Could you please not call me ma'am? My name is Beth." I wasn't at all surprised by his next response.

"Oh I am so sorry ma'am. I mean Beth. Could you tell me the patient's name please?"

I repeated my mantra to myself. *God get me through this. God get me through this. God get me through this...* "Her name is Ellen Harris; and to recap, Dr. Hart's nurse faxed the order Tuesday around 10:00 a.m. When will Margaret be back from lunch?"

There was dead silence like poor Andy was afraid to speak. "She won't be back until around 2:00. It's her birthday so her co-workers took her out to lunch."

I dropped my head and moved the iced tea behind my neck. *God get me through this, God get me through this, God get me through this...*

"Look, Andy. I need this bed delivered ASAP. Is it possible that the delivery guy might have a cell phone? Could we call him?" My head had been pounding for a couple of hours. I wasn't sure if it was the heat or the stress of making these arrangements, but suddenly my eyes were fixated on the box of Tylenol sitting at the edge of my tray.

"Oh, that's a good idea. Let me see if I can find the number." Andy sounded a bit relieved. Again I heard him riffling through papers; then he picked up the phone. "Uh, Beth? I need to put you on hold."

Before I could object, "HOME HOSPITAL CARE. WHEN YOU BRING A LOVED ONE HOME BE PREPARED. WE SUPPLY OXYGEN, HOSPITAL BEDS, COMMODES…"

Frantically and with the help of my teeth, I tore open the gigantic box of Tylenol. I jabbed a pencil through the foil and made a big hole, then popped two pills into my mouth, took a sip of the iced tea, threw my head back and swallowed. I needed to go downstairs for more ice, but I heard Andy.

"Uh, Beth? Good news. I found the delivery guy's number."

I sighed a huge sigh. "Oh thank God. What did he say? Where is he?"

"Oh, I didn't call him yet."

My blood simmered but I made the effort to be nice. "Wellllll Andy, perhaps you could give him a call or give me the number and I will call him."

"I'll call him now. Please ho…" This time he didn't even get the entire last word out before he pushed that damn hold button.

"HOME HOSPITAL CARE. WHEN YOU BRING A LOVED ONE HOME BE PREPARED. WE SUPPLY…" The game-show voice went on and on and I knew this would take a while, so I went downstairs to the kitchen for more ice. The freezer was cool and I wanted to stay there all day but I had to get back to my commode in case Andy

Andy had more questions. I filled the glass, popped a cube in my mouth, rubbed one on my forehead and one between my drenched breasts, then headed back upstairs. I let my cat Toes in on the way. I picked up the phone just as Andy answered.

"Uh, Beth?"

"Yes Andy. Good news?"

"Did you order a commode with that hospital bed?" Oh My God!

"What? Are you freakin' kidding me? No I didn't order a commode. In fact I'm sitting on a commode, Andy! Just the bed and air flow mattress." I inhaled. *Deep breaths, deep breaths.* "What did the delivery guy say?"

"I didn't get a chance to talk to him because he's on his break and he turns his cell phone off while he eats his lunch. I left him a message to call as soon as possible."

Toes jumped up on one end of the tray and slid right off the other end, taking the opened bottle of Tylenol and remaining papers with him. Pills scattered everywhere. Toes was in a playful mood and I was not. He jumped back up and stuck his muzzle in my glass of iced tea, but when the fan oscillated in his direction he hissed at it and jumped down. I reached for a large box of Depends and hurriedly tried to open it with one hand but I stopped dead when I heard Andy ask, "What is the address on this order?"

"Is this some sort of joke? I can't believe this! The address is 3 Dear Meadow Lane." I struggled to open up the large box of adult diapers. "I know you are trying your best, Andy, but that hospital bed has to be here within an hour and you can't find the paperwork!" I continued the fight with the diaper box and finally it ripped open crudely and about ten diapers flew out. I picked one up. "Does Margaret have a cell phone? Do you have her number?"

Andy was quick to answer. "Yes she does, but we have strict orders to only use it in emergencies."

"WELL WHAT THE HELL DO YOU THINK THIS IS, ANDY??? CALL HER NOW!" I unfolded a diaper, held it over the floor and poured some cold iced tea and a couple of ice cubes into it. Then I wrapped it around my neck and secured it with the sticky tabs. It was all I could think of to cool down my body and my anger.

"Okay I'll call her right now. Hold on..."

"No please don't put me on..." Too late.

"HOME HOSPITAL CARE. WHEN YOU BRING A LOVED..." *God get me through this. God get me through this.*

Toes had discovered the ninety-eight pills that spilled and was batting them all over the hardwood floor. I wasn't sure which sound was more annoying, the game-show voice or the pills rolling from one end of the room to the other.

"Uh, Beth?"

"Yes? You better have good news because I'm getting pretty pissed off here and you don't want to piss off a menopausal woman in the middle of a heat wave, Andy. Do ya know what I mean?"

I heard a very timid voice. "Uh, Beth?"

"Like the guy says, I AM bringing a loved one home and trying to be prepared, but you are making it really difficult, Andy, really difficult."

"Uh, Beth?"

"Do I have to come over and pick the damn bed up myself?"

"Beth?"

"What Andy, what?"

"The delivery guy called and said he was running late and that he'll be there any minute."

Just then I heard the doorbell and yelled, "Who is it?"

"Home Hospital Care."

I held my hand over the phone and yelled downstairs. "Do you have a hospital bed?"

"Yes ma'am."

"Come upstairs."

I spoke gently to Andy.

"He's here. I'm sorry I was so cranky. I know you did your best and I appreciate it. You've been very patient. Thank you, Andy."

"Sorry for the delay, Beth."

"Bye Andy."

A voice yelled up to me.

"Ma'am did you order a commode with this?"

I put my head face down on the tray, and tea from my diapered neck dripped over the few remaining papers. *God get me through this. God get me through this, God get me through this...*

CHAPTER 1

Bob and Joanne lived right next door to us. He was tall and slender with chiseled features. Joanne was beautiful with a sexy figure that was enhanced by the wide belts and fitted styles of the 50s. My sister Janet and I shared a bedroom, and our window faced their bedroom window. Every night Mama tucked us in, kissed us good night, and closed the blinds. Together in low voices we counted her footsteps descend the fifteen stairs until we knew the coast was clear.

Then Janet scrambled out of bed and got Susan, our oldest sister, while I scrambled out of bed and opened the blinds. The three of us sat there on my bed in the dark and watched Joanne and Bob parade naked around their well-lit bedroom until they fell into bed. They made sounds that, as a five-year-old, I didn't understand but could tell that they seemed to enjoy themselves. We watched Joanne and Bob conceive five children—which later turned out to be quite lucrative in babysitting jobs.

I was the youngest of three girls. We lived with our parents in a beautiful two-story brick house on a street lined with magnificent maple and elm trees in Ann Arbor, Michigan. For the most part we got along. My childhood was perfect. Our house was perfect. Our neighborhood was perfect. Dad was perfect. Mom was perfect. The cats were perfect. (Except for the times they used to pee in the dining room corners and Dad would holler, "Those Goddamn cats! I wish I was treated as well as a Harris cat!")

Dad was an engineer. He designed wheel covers for cars, and on Friday nights we ate popcorn out of the prototypes. Everybody wanted to hang out at our house. Dad entertained us (and my many friends) with jokes and stories, and he made everything fun, from raking leaves to shoveling snow. If any of us girls had a sore throat, he took our pulse, lathered a sock with Vicks VapoRub, and secured it around our neck with a huge safety pin; then he stayed with us and read stories until we fell asleep. If one of us was too sick to go to Mass, Dad stayed home and said Mass in his underwear while scrambled eggs burned on the stove. A piece of crispy bacon placed on our tongue served as the Communion host.

When I was in the second grade I stuttered so bad I couldn't recite the Hail Mary. It took forever to get it out. "Hail M-M-M-M… ary…" I couldn't say any word that began with *M* or *B*, which was awful because my name is Mary Beth. The other students rolled their eyes when it was my turn, and I remember Bucky Straub saying, "Aww man, this is gonna take forever."

Mama, realizing that my disorder was here to stay, sought out a child psychologist for me when I was in the fourth grade. To this day I appreciate Mama's sensitivity, because if I was the least bit uncomfortable with any of them she would say, "Don't worry dear, we'll find the right one." And she did. By the time I was in fifth grade she had found Mrs. Shoecraft. I felt safe with her and I looked forward to our meetings. Every Friday I was allowed to leave school fifteen minutes early to go to the clinic. Mrs. Shoecraft finally told my parents to get me out of Catholic school. Back in the 50s, Catholics took being Catholic VERY seriously. It was a big deal. But not such a big deal to Mom and Dad that what was best for me didn't come first to them. I muddled through the rest of St. Francis because I only had one year left there, and they thought it would be harder on me to go to a new school at that point. I remember them discussing it over and over whether to move me or not. So in seventh grade I went to public school. I don't think many Catholic parents would have chosen that option in those days, but it was the best decision that Mom and Dad made. I excelled. I was the lead in plays and addressed the student body as if I had never had the speech disorder. I found my voice there and nobody has been able to shut me up since.

Mama was an artist, and in the middle of the 60s, her free spirit was desperate to fly. She painted exquisite floral paintings, portraits, and still lifes, and was one of the original founders of the now famous Ann Arbor Street Art Fair. Conflict began to brew when Dad insisted that she continue to attend Detroit Lions football games with him and the office couples. After years of saying yes to the games, yes to the wild office parties (which Dad was always the life of), and yes to late-night dinners, Mama finally refused. She wanted to paint in peace with no distractions, to be independent. And she wanted to live alone. So about the time I started college in 1968, Mama moved to a small apartment in the quaint little nearby town of Chelsea. Eventually she sold enough paintings to buy a little A-frame down the road from her apartment. It was in the woods, and she spent her days outside painting by the pond or on a hilltop blanketed with wildflowers. Mama never wanted to cut any of her family out of her life; she just wanted to follow her passion.

Then Mama discovered the *Course in Miracles,* which is a self-study in achieving spiritual transformation based on the practice of forgiveness. The philosophy is: "Nothing real can be threatened. Nothing unreal exists. Herein lies the peace of God." With the Course, Mama finally met kindred spirits who inspired her and appreciated her art and her intellect. She was invited to art openings, symphonies, and one party in particular where she met Louise, who was visiting from San Bernardino, California and adored Mama from the start.

Louise told Mama about the little seaside town of Carmel-by-the-Sea in California. Carmel was founded by a group of Bohemian artists and had a most impressive art association. Louise looked at Mama's paintings and encouraged her to live in a place where flowers bloom year round. A move to California was Mama's main focus. She researched the protocol for submission into the Carmel Art Association, and with Dad's help she spent her days photographing all of her paintings.

So it was Mama's devotion to art that compelled her to pack up her little red Ford Pinto, drive to California, and submit her work into The Carmel Art Association. The jury accepted her on her first submission.

In the meantime, I had dropped out of college, moved back to Ann Arbor, and gotten a job in the registrar's office at the University of Michigan. I became depressed and often called in sick, until one day when I went into work, they fired me. I walked the streets of Ann Arbor and saw a sign in a travel agency that said, "Detroit/Amsterdam/Detroit, Six Weeks, $159.00."

I needed an adventure. So the following Monday I was on my way to Europe with $5.00 in my pocket. I hitchhiked from Amsterdam to Brindisi, Italy, where I caught a ferry to Greece, then hitched to Vai on the northeast coast of Crete. There was nothing there but a gorgeous beach and commune living with people from all over the world. We combined our food and slept under the stars.

The trip changed my life. It gave me the confidence and desire to move out of Ann Arbor. Mama had taken a job in a dress shop in downtown Carmel and her apartment was within walking distance. Her paintings were in the Carmel Art Association in addition to a local gallery, and her social life was thriving. Why not move to California? I packed up my Datsun 240Z, grabbed the cat, and off I went.

The beauty of Carmel astounded me. I had never seen anything like it. While sitting on Carmel Beach's soft white sand, a local guy sitting near me said, "There's a whale." I thought he was joking. "Shut up. I may be from Michigan but I'm not gullible."

"No, really. Look out there and watch for spouts." I strained my eyes, and within a minute, sure enough I saw a spout, then the shiny back, and then the fluke. Seconds later there was another spout. It took my breath away. I wanted to share it with my big sister. I called Susan.

"Get out here. This place is amazing." Within weeks Susan had left her boyfriend and was on her way.

Mama decided that Carmel was where she wanted to settle, so she sold her beloved A-frame in the woods in Michigan. It turned out that a friend of Susan's wanted to buy it, so it never had to go on the market. Mama, Susan and I went in search of a new house.

After Mama bought a modest house in the Mission Fields area of Carmel, we felt bad that Dad, who adored his family, was still alone in the big, perfect house back in Ann Arbor. Janet, our middle sister, was living in Texas at the time with her husband who was in the army. Months later I flew back to Michigan and helped him prepare our perfect house to sell. By 1979, most of our family was together in California.

CHAPTER 2

My free spirit was fluttering its wings again. Since I had hitchhiked through Europe to Greece, the travel bug had bitten me and I craved a new adventure. I was happy with my family close by but bored with my life. Waitressing?? Really?? There had to be something bigger and better for me. Mama tried to console me with the *Course in Miracles'* philosophy. "But dear, The Course says none of this is real. This life is just an illusion." *Oh, The Course says, The Course says, The Course says… I am so over the damn Course.* Poor Mama.

I read in our local paper that there was an ethnographic film series going on in a nearby University town, Santa Cruz, which reminded me of Ann Arbor. I missed living in a University town where there is constant stimulation and always something exciting going on, whether it is street musicians, rallies, or protests. I attended the showing of Margaret Mead and Gregory Bateson's film, *Trance and Dance in Bali,* which they shot in the 1930s. The film made a huge impact. I had to go there. I approached the guy responsible for the film series, and it turned out that he was a filmmaker also deeply moved by the film and had spent many months in Bali. He had hours of footage and asked me if I would like to see some of it. "Are you kidding me? Where and when?" Steve came over and spent several days with me until he was off to Bali again. My life became consumed with how I would save up enough money for a $1000.00 plane ticket plus living expenses. I took a second job selling Jag jeans and started stashing my waitressing tips in a jar.

Every evening the sunset drew me to the beach like a magnet. One particular night was no exception. I was determined to hang on to my Bali vision but I couldn't raise the money. Frustrated, I sat and had a harsh conversation with God. "You're really beginning to piss me off. Why are you making this so difficult? And don't tell me that it's not meant to be because I know it is. Would it kill ya to just throw me a bone here? I'm willing to work my ass off, but doing what?? I'm so tired of struggling." Well, I'll be damned if He didn't respond. The moment I said I was tired of struggling, he said, "then stop struggling." And I got it.

It was so obvious!! *Put on an ethnographic film series yourself!* I called Steve just before he left for Bali, and he gave me contacts and numbers. I found the perfect venue in a small music hall at the community college. Every

Friday for four weeks I showed a different topic: Trance and Dance, Healers, Music, Masks. I had flyers made up, talked on radio programs, and called everybody I knew. It was a huge success. The place was packed all four weeks. BUT the biggest moneymaker for me was the cheesecake I sold during intermission. Each day, I made three cheesecakes with chocolate swirls and sold them by the slice.

I gave up my apartment and moved in with Mom and Dad because I planned to be away for two months. On December 15, 1980, I was on a plane to Bali. They drove me to San Francisco Airport and I hopped on a plane around midnight. Mama was supportive from the start and slipped me two hundred dollars in a floral fabric-bound journal. She had also safety pinned a Holy Scapular inside my suitcase which read, "Whosoever dies wearing this Scapular Shall not suffer eternal fire!" and threw a bunch of wet wipes in my carry-on, which I didn't discover until I arrived.

Something else I discovered upon arrival was an entry from Mama in the journal: *There is a light in you that cannot die; whose presence is so holy that the world is sanctified because of you. All things that live bring gifts to you, and offer them in gratitude and gladness at your feet. The scent of flowers is their gift to you. The waves bow down before you, and the trees extend their arms to shield you from the heat, and lay their leaves before you on the ground that you may walk in softness, while the wind sinks to a whisper round your holy head. The light in you is what the universe longs to behold. All living things are still before you, for they recognize Who walks with you. The light you carry is their own. And thus they see in you their holiness, saluting you as Savior and as God. Accept their reverence, for it is due to Holiness Itself that walks with you, transforming in its gentle Light all things unto Its likeness and Its purity. XO*

I stepped off the plane in Bali—and my soul was home. The warm tropical air instantly enveloped me like a mother embraces her newborn. I had never before seen palm trees loaded with coconuts. If you observe Balinese dance, you realize that the finger movements resemble the palm fronds when the breeze blows through them. I knew this would not be my last trip to Bali. I had to figure out how to live there, but I didn't fast forward and struggle to find an answer. I absorbed each second to the fullest and trusted that the answer would find me. I had an island to explore.

The Balinese people are poor, yet creative, calm, gentle, and fulfilled. I had wonderful, poignant conversations with my Balinese friend, Nyoman. In her broken English and my broken Indonesian, we would talk long into the balmy, tropical evenings under brilliant moons and millions of stars. Together we solved the world's problems.

During one of our conversations, her grandfather approached us. His skin was tanned and wrinkled from years of working in the rice paddies, and his withered cheeks were so sunken that his face resembled a mushroom. He wore a weathered baseball cap that was so old I couldn't make out the logo. His tattered Rolling Stones t-shirt was faded and had many holes, and the sarong he wore around his tiny hips looked ancient. Its once vivid batik pattern was dulled from years of having been scrubbed with a rock in the river.

He squatted and sucked on a clove cigarette, which sparked with each puff. Then he looked up at me and said, "Dari America?" (Are you from America?)

I lowered my head and answered, "Yes."

Then he said, "In America, you…" as he shot his hand up to the sky and looked into space, then pointed to the moon. I looked at my friend Nyoman for assurance and said, "Yes, in America we go to moon."

Then he said, "In America, children die *tidak makanan*."

Oh God, I knew where he was going with this. *Makanan* translates to food and *tidak* means no. I told him that yes, there is starvation in America and children die every day.

He lowered his head and nodded sideways, took another drag off his cigarette, then looked up at me and said, "Then why this?" And he shot his hand and arm up towards the moon again. "It costs money, no"?

I had no answer.

In Bali I discovered an astounding clothing designer named Kiyo. I'm not sure if he was American or Canadian, but he was a genius ahead of his time. His cotton pants, jackets, shirts, and dresses were brilliant colors and they all turned into something. Pants turned into backpacks, dresses turned into duffle bags, and so on. I invested what little money I had and purchased a bundle of clothes to take home to sell to friends who hosted parties. The parties were quite a success, and before I knew it I was back in Bali and eager to find Kiyo. Back and forth I went, each time investing a little more money, and each time making more money. Every time I returned home from Bali, my only focus was how and when to get back there.

My family was still very precious to me, however. Mom and Dad seemed to be doing well. Dad did anything he could to support Mom's painting and she appreciated his efforts. In the spring Dad took her for long drives, and together they discovered where the wildflowers were most plentiful. There were moments I'm sure when they wanted to distance themselves from each other, but in the big picture of life they were growing old together and doing more for each other.

It was time to find my own place to live. Mom and Dad were happy to have me there, but I was thirty and it was time to be independent. I put the word out, and within hours a friend of Susan's called me and said she had a friend looking for a nanny to live in their guesthouse. This person was Shary Farr. Shary used to come into the restaurant where I worked, put her baby, Jessica, snuggled in a basket, on the oyster bar and, order food to go. She was as nice and sweet as a person could be, with the biggest, bluest, most soulful eyes any human could possibly have. She was polite, kind, and gentle with an ever-glowing aura. In fact, when Shary turned her back towards me I looked for wings. I was happy at the prospect of getting to know her, and although I was apprehensive about committing to a position when I still felt married to Bali, I took the position and moved into her guesthouse.

When I was in Bali I missed Shary and Jessica in

California, and when I was in California I missed Bali. Jessie became another granddaughter to Mom and Dad. They only lived about a mile apart, and even when I was away, they remained close and Mom and Dad included her in any family gatherings.

After three years I grew weary of going back and forth. Visas were harder to extend, Bali was getting crowded, developers from Java were moving in, and the coral was dying. It was time to put the suitcase to the back of the closet. I was homesick. I didn't want to just visit my family—I wanted to be a part of it. Mom and Dad were getting older and I longed to go to my niece Christine's ballet recitals and Christmas pageants. I didn't want her to grow up without me. I wanted to laugh with my sisters and not get on a plane the next day. And I wanted to live in the Farr's guesthouse and wake up with Jessie curled next to me and have coffee with Shary in our nightgowns 'til noon. Bali had run its course.

Life in the Farr's guesthouse was pure joy. Jessie and I were best pals, and Shary and I were best friends. We would sit in her dining room as the morning sun poured through its many windows and talk for hours. We talked about spirituality, read Tarot cards, visualized what we wanted to happen, and threw the Runes. We went to listen to Elizabeth Kubler Ross, Ram Das, and Dan Millman speak. We meditated every day, and I told Shary about the time I astral projected in her guesthouse (well, out of her guesthouse). We read Shirley MacLaine's *Out on a Limb* and all the books about life after death and life after life and death after life. We were fascinated with channelers and wondered whether or not Ramtha was for real. We spent a fortune on psychics. Then we'd go shopping and argue over who was the sexiest man alive.

The downside of being a nanny is that the kid grows up. Jessie was around nine when she came into her social scene. I had friends in L.A. that I frequently visited, and I became enthralled with that area. A part of me yearned to be an entertainer, but it's kind of hard when you have no talent. Still, I was fascinated with the industry. So as Jessie grew older and not so much in need of a nanny, I toyed with the idea of moving to L.A. Okay, I more than toyed—I moved.

CHAPTER 3

For two years I struggled from one job to another in the entertainment industry. The highlight of my less-than-stellar career was when I worked as a production assistant. This particular job was a safety belt commercial starring four celebrity legends: Charles Nelson Reilly, Phyllis Diller, and to be honest, I have no memory of who the other two were. I do remember that I was thrilled to meet Phyllis Diller.

When we broke for lunch I insisted on delivering Ms. Diller's meal to her trailer. My heart pounded as I knocked on the door of one of the greatest comedic icons that ever lived.

"Miss Diller, your lunch is ready."

"Come in. Please come in." By the sound of the voice, there was no doubt that it was the great Phyllis Diller. I balanced a Styrofoam plate piled high with fried chicken, cole slaw, and French fries covered with aluminum foil as

I entered her trailer. There she was in her streaked fright wig and thick, black false eyelashes, wearing an outrageous polyester outfit splashed with a loud print. I sat her plate down on her makeup table then turned to leave. It was a rule to not interact with celebrities.

"Where are you going"?

I told her that I was going to eat my lunch on the set while the crew was gone. "Can you get your lunch and eat it with me?"

I didn't care if I ever worked in that town again. What a fabulous offer!

"Really?" I couldn't believe my ears.

"Well of course, please join me."

"I'll go grab it and be right back." I was so thrilled I lost my appetite but went to the caterer and grabbed the first thing I saw. I briskly walked back to the trailer and on the way spotted the director.

"Phyllis Diller has asked me join her for lunch."

"She's great, isn't she?" he replied.

I gave a courtesy knock on her door, then entered. She ate the chicken leg with her fingers, then moved her lunch aside to make room for mine, but I placed it on my lap. I didn't take the foil off my plate because I decided to delay eating and go out on a limb. You never know how intimate to get with celebrities or if you should speak to them at all, but I was compelled to tell her something. I thought about it for about five seconds before I took the risk and just went for it. "I have a story I would love to share with you." She looked up from her chicken with a puzzled but interested look on her face. Her eyes widened and she gave me a nod of approval.

"I was about six or seven years old so it was around 1956 or 1957. Our family was gathered around the television set to watch what else but *The Ed Sullivan Show.* I think it was your first appearance. One joke you told made my mom laugh so hard that she ran out of the room, and when she stood up there was a little spot of pee where she had been sitting. You made my mom pee on the chair! And she had just had it re-upholstered!"

Phyllis threw her head back and gave out her uproarious signature laugh. A laugh so great that I have no idea how to describe it other than "that Phyllis Diller laugh." Then she looked at me intently and asked if I remembered the joke.

"I DO remember the joke."

She put her chicken leg down and listened.

"You had just married Fang and it was your first Thanksgiving as a wife. You had no idea how to make a turkey. So you called your best friend and asked her what to do. She told you that you had to first dress the turkey before you roasted it. With your long cigarette holder in your hand and wearing that short, shiny dress, you looked into the camera and said, "Well it took me two weeks just to make the blouse." Both of us roared. I could tell that I had made Phyllis Diller's day.

Again she threw her head back and laughed that raucous laugh. "Thank you so much for telling me that."

"Thank you for bringing laughter to the world. You are

a treasure. I can't wait to tell my mother that I had lunch with you. I have to go now. You will be wanted on the set in about fifteen minutes. Thank you again."

I walked back to the sound stage with my food untouched and dialed Mama's number.

"Hello?"

"Hey Mama! Are you sitting down? You'll never guess who I just had lunch with."

As thrilled as Mama was about my lunch with Phyllis Diller, she informed me that she had fallen and broken a hip.

"Why didn't you call me? I would have come home!"

"We didn't want to take you from your work, dear. You have worked so hard to get to where you are, and your father has been wonderful."

"When did this happen?"

"Oh it's been about a week now. I'm healing nicely. We are managing okay. I don't want you to worry."

I drove to Carmel several times during Mama's healing, loaded with goodies from Trader Joe's to relieve Dad and spend time with them. When I was sure she was out of the woods, I dove back into my work in L.A. For several months I lived the high life: drinking expensive champagne, riding in stretch limos, hobnobbing with celebrities, and attending fabulous parties in opulent homes. I climbed the ladder to success and I was about three quarters of the way up—but on my way to what? Stroking actors' egos? Settling quibbles between who got the biggest trailer? My priorities felt challenged. I had met some wonderful people whose friendships I will cherish forever, but for the most part I felt as if my free spirit's wings had been clipped.

When I lived in Bali, no one was in a hurry, and sex was leisurely and would go on for hours. In the background were the gentle sounds of island life: palms swaying in the wind and an occasional coconut falling to the ground with a thud; geckos smack smack smacking on the walls, and insects continually buzzing around. Tropical thunderstorms added exciting energy, and the shimmering sounds of the gamelan were accompanied by children's laughter.

In L.A. it was another story. We were always in a hurry, and you had to schedule sex.

"Where are you shooting today?"

"Shooting a Budweiser commercial on Zuma beach. Six a.m. call. Then I have to have dinner with the client. Gotta go. Love ya, bye."

I had less free time, and when I did have time off, I worried about a job I was working on, or a future job, or the job that was over but that would have repercussions because someone or something had screwed up. I craved a walk on Carmel Beach and I missed Shary and Jessie. This L.A. lifestyle wasn't where my soul longed to be.

I had worked at the same production company for about two years. Then one day I received two phone calls that put my life on a collision course. One was a conference call from my director and my producer. They planned to groom me for a future position as executive producer. This was a huge offer. WOW! I could buy a house and hire someone to clean it. I could take Mama to Giverney. She always wanted to see the Monet Gardens. I was going to make tons of money. My free spirit could stay in a cage for a while. As I picked up the phone to call Mom and Dad, it suddenly rang with an incoming call from my sister Susan. When we hung up, I was faced with the biggest decision of my life—but there was really no choice.

The doctor had discovered a tumor at the base of Dad's liver and it was untreatable. Mama's hip and hands were stricken with rheumatoid arthritis. It was so severe in her hands that she could no longer hold a paintbrush. I refused the job promotion, packed up my Honda, grabbed my dog Scout, bid good-bye to Hollywood, and moved back to Carmel.

CHAPTER 4

When I returned to Carmel, the situation was worse than I'd realized. The arthritis had ravaged both of Mom's hips, and her hands were deformed. Dad's tumor created internal bleeding so the doctors had inserted a stent to direct the blood flow. It wasn't a permanent cure and he had several endoscopies to cauterize small amounts of blood that gathered in his esophagus. We never found out if the tumor was malignant; it was untreatable, so we opted to not put Dad through a biopsy. In spite of his possible cancer, Dad experienced no pain and continued to play golf and take care of Mama.

I took a part-time job at a small record company in Carmel and moved into a studio apartment a few streets away. One day in March it started to rain, then storm, then hail. Strong winds came up, followed by thunder and lightning. As I sat at my desk, I heard a loud, jolting crack.

A huge tree had fallen in Devendorf Park and uprooted ten feet of sidewalk. Shortly after that, Dad called to let me know he and Mama were being evacuated as soon as possible because the levy had broken and water was headed their way. *My elderly parents were being forced out of their home in Mission Fields, which was near the river.* "Gather as much as you can and don't forget Mama's meds," I said. "I'm on my way."

It took months of grueling, intense labor to clean up from that flood. Mom and Dad stayed out at Susan's while she and I spent twelve cold, drenched hours a day for weeks in toxic mud cleaning and sorting what we could. With fires, everything is gone. But in a flood, you are faced with the decision of what is salvageable and what isn't. If it's worth saving, then you spend hours scrubbing and disinfecting everything. In our case, the saddest part of all was the loss of many of Mama's paintings.

Although Dad's health was declining, he continued to be the contractor. He said, "I need to stay alive long enough to get your mother back in her comfortable home."

And that he did. They moved back home in November. I moved in with them because Dad now faced his own health issues and needed help getting to doctor appointments and fixing meals. I moved into the small bedroom between their rooms. Mama was an avid PBS fan and often watched concerts. Dad was a shoot 'em up cowboy kinda guy and loved westerns. Neither one of them could hear worth a damn, so imagine: The Three Tenors full volume from one wall, and gunfights at the

O.K. Corral full volume from the other wall. Even my dog Scout tried to muffle the sounds by crawling under the covers. Where do you draw the line on compassion?

We lost Dad on March 23, 1996, exactly a year after the flood.

CHAPTER 5

Mama loved birds. She placed feeders in every tree and birdbaths throughout the yard, and hung sugar water outside the kitchen window. When we sat outside it delighted her so to watch a hummingbird flit from blossom to blossom and drink sweet nectar from flowers that she grew in her own garden. Mama reminded me of a little bird herself—sweet, delicate, beautiful and harmless. And like a bird that brings great joy with its songs, Mama brought great joy to many with her art.

One day Mama and I sat in her bedroom and listened to a mockingbird sing for hours as it sat on a telephone wire. We held back laughter each time the bird threw its little head back and changed its melody and voice as it imitated other birds.

Before arthritis incapacitated Mama, she had gone out to her backyard and snipped a small branch off an attractive little Modesto Ash tree that she had planted years before. The branch had no leaves but many little limbs. It was about four feet wide and three feet from top to bottom, and it was extremely awkward to handle. She placed ten small life-like blue, red, yellow, and gray birds on different limbs, and hung the branch over the mantle. The display was captivating, and everybody that entered the room smiled and commented on it. When a fire glowed in the fireplace and candles were lit, the shadow of the branch with its little birds projected twice its size and it was enchanting. Years later that branch would play a major role in our lives.

As Mama's pain increased, so did her medications. By now she took at least ten prescriptions a day plus various vitamins and supplements, with no positive results from anything. She needed assistance to the bathroom, and she could no longer shower herself, feed herself, or dress herself. In spite of her weight loss, she felt heavier when I lifted her, and it was difficult for her to stand by herself.

I didn't mind the grocery shopping, cooking, cleaning, laundry, and waiting in long lines for new medications. I didn't mind sitting up with her in the middle of the night praying that the pain would miraculously go away. I minded that this was my mother and I felt helpless.

Shary Farr still lived close by and our friendship continued to blossom. Her grandmother had taught her about end-of-life planning when she was very young, and Shary knew that this was her calling. She started a business providing guidance to families of the elderly or ill. Shary met with the families, assessed what their needs were, and advised them. She was on the board of the local hospice house, gave talks at Community Hospital of Monterey and other hospitals, and was familiar with of all the care facilities on the Monterey Peninsula. She had a network of caregivers, but when necessary she stepped in herself. Shary was my biggest supporter and we spoke every day.

"Shary, I am so exhausted I don't know where to turn." I was teary eyed.

"Beth, I know you love your mom, but it may be time to think about placing her. You're doing a great job with her but…"

"NO Shary, I can do this. I know I can."

"Beth, you're exhausted and your mom is only going to get worse."

I continued the argument. "All I have to do is get her meds straightened out and she'll be better."

Shary's voice was calm and gentle. "Beth, your mom isn't safe with you anymore. Please, just think about it."

I told Shary that I would think about it, then stuck my head back in the sand.

CHAPTER 6

"Your mother is no longer safe with you. You must place her in a home."

"No doctor! I don't believe it. I won't do it!"

The rheumatoid arthritis had crippled both Mama's hands and feet, and excruciating pain from osteoporosis was settling into her spine as well. OxyContin was her primary painkiller; and as a result, she lost weight, hallucinated, became paranoid, and lay awake most nights sobbing in pain as I held her. We tried pain specialists, arthritis specialists, osteoporosis specialists, and prayer, but nothing worked. I had moved in three months before that to take care of my precious parents, and now I felt helpless caring for Mama. Because of her behavior on the medications, her doctor had diagnosed her with having dementia or the beginning of Alzheimer's. Now the doctor wanted to put her in a skilled nursing facility, and I was horrified.

"What? She doesn't have dementia or Alzheimer's. She's clearly overmedicated. My God, you have her on fifteen pills a day. How can you be so sure?"

His response was, "If you want her pain to be managed, then we have no choice but to increase the painkillers as her pain increases. Now with the new signs of dementia, we'll have to prescribe something to control that."

I was stunned. "PRESCRIBE SOMETHING TO CONTROL THAT? ARE YOU FREAKIN' KIDDING ME??? MORE MEDS? I can't believe I am hearing that you want to pump her full of even more drugs! First of all, Mama does NOT have dementia, and second, she is ALREADY OVERMEDICATED."

"I'm afraid she does have the beginning of dementia and I..."

"SHE DOES NOT HAVE DEMENTIA!"

The doctor took my hand. "Look, I know this is hard for you to accept, but you must understand that she is eighty-eight years old and it is not uncommon for some..."

I yanked my hand back. "Look, Doctor, nobody knows her, loves her, or understands her better than I do; and I am telling you that you need to get her off some of the meds and she will be herself again. You can't just write her off and keep prescribing more drugs. I know she's in there. I just know it." Tears welled up in my eyes and I wasn't sure if it was from sadness or frustration. "There must be another way to control her pain, Doctor, there just has to be."

"We can try new painkillers that are on the market, but either way she is too much for you to handle by yourself now. You are losing the rest you need to take care of her. I am sorry."

I felt like a failure.

He went on. "What you're doing for your mom is heroic. But her hands are unable to hold onto anything anymore, she can barely stand by herself, and she cannot walk without assistance. For her safety, you have to let her go."

I began to surrender. I realized then just how exhausted I was. "If I choose to place her, it's going to be an assisted living home. I will not put her in a skilled nursing facility." I had done my homework and knew what to expect.

The difference between assisted living homes and skilled nursing facilities is huge. Assisted living homes are in houses so there are fewer residents, usually no more than six. There are living rooms and dining rooms, and the bedrooms are private. You can bring in your own furniture, television, phone, decorations, and belongings. Generally, they are in neighborhoods where there are gardens and trees. The staff is "hands-on" and the food is home cooked. But residents must be able to walk without assistance, and bathe and dress themselves.

Skilled nursing facilities are hospitals. There can be anywhere from fifty to one hundred fifty patients. The sounds in some of these facilities include people yelling from fear and moaning in pain. Some people are so drugged up that they're just existing and barely aware of anything. The nursing facilities often smell of Pine Sol and urine, and they always appear to be short-staffed. Many of the patients, sadly, have been abandoned by their families and are scared or overmedicated or both. These places can be impersonal and very depressing.

The doctor reassured me that some assisted living homes are now licensed to take one immobile patient. I told him I would call Shary and start the search, but then I wanted to get Mama off as many meds as I could.

Shortly after that, OxyContin appeared on the cover of *Time* magazine. Turns out Mama was not the only one overdosing on OxyContin. Kids were using it as a recreational party drug and often ended up in the emergency room and in some cases, dead.

I was overwhelmed, frustrated, exhausted, confused, and sad. I tried desperately to find caregivers to help me, but they never worked out. And it was difficult for my sisters to pitch in. Susan drove an hour each way to a stressful job and had a huge garden that required constant work. And she was married. Janet was divorced, worked full time as a preschool teacher in San Jose, and she was justifiably exhausted by the weekends. I was completely alone and lonely.

My sacred place to go whenever I had a meltdown was Dad's tool shed that he had built behind the house. The roof was yellow corrugated fiberglass and it was always warm and light inside. It smelled of sawdust and paint thinner and there were old photos of us that Dad had hung over his saws and grinders and wheel covers. Even though he had passed on two years before, I depended on his energy and felt safe there as if he were holding me in his arms again. It was my sanctuary.

One day while snooping in the shed I found a box of letters. In it was a card with a mama cat and kittens on the front that I had written to Mama in 1973 after she moved to California from her home in Michigan where she and Dad had lived for thirty years. I still lived in Michigan at the time I wrote the card. It was a sweet, loving card, and at the end I had written, "As long as I am alive, Mama, I promise you will never go into a nursing home." Where did that come from? Mama wasn't sick then, and it wasn't something that we ever discussed. I was only in my twenties, and who thinks of long-term health care in their twenties? Now I had to break that promise to Mama and it broke my heart. I didn't want to give her up. Nobody could take care of her the way I could. Nobody knew her as well as I did, but I felt I had no choice but to give up control. Mama was no longer safe with me.

CHAPTER 7

How was I going to tell Mama that we were about to take her out of her home and place her in a facility where strangers would take care of her? I wasn't convinced that she would even understand, because as the pain in her spine intensified, the medication was increased.

With Shary's help, we found a nice assisted-living facility in downtown Carmel called Cypress Manor. It was close to her house and right around the corner from the clothing shop where I worked two days a week.

Apprehensively, I approached Mama's room, knelt beside her bed, and took her hand.

"Mama, the doctor says I can't take care of you anymore." I caught her at a moment when there was a window of clarity in her foggy state of mind. She looked at me. Only a part of my mama existed in her drugged stupor. "Tomorrow we are going to take you to an assisted living facility to see if you like it. If you don't we will keep looking until we find the right one." She turned her head and a tear rolled down her cheek onto the pillow.

"I understand darling. I don't want to be a burden to you any longer. If you think that is the right decision then I will go."

"But if you have any doubts about this place then we will find another one, I promise. It is thirty seconds from the shop where I'm working, so I can visit every day before work and after work. Susan will stop by on her way home too. I hear the food is very good."

"I will do whatever you think is best." I didn't know what was best. Mama had no fight in her. She surrendered graciously and courageously.

There wasn't much wall space in Cypress Manor, but Susan and I decided that we should find a place for Mama's beloved bird branch. We chose a spot above the television. I climbed up on the TV table and held the branch in place while Susan tried to attach it with pushpins. The pushpins were too short so the branch fell behind the TV and some of the twigs snapped off. We pulled out the table, grabbed the branch, and attempted to hang the branch again. Mama looked on with delight and was pleased that we thought of bringing the branch. Once again I climbed up on the table and held the branch in place. Susan had gone downstairs and asked for some nails and a hammer. We tried several times to secure the branch, but it was so awkward that it kept falling behind the table. In frustration Susan said, "Oh let's forget about the damn branch for now!"

"No! No way are we NOT going to hang this damn branch. Why don't you go see if Kathryn has some longer nails?" Susan headed downstairs while I continued to hold the branch in place.

Kathryn was the housekeeper and cook. She was Black and from the Deep South. She was fun and calm and usually sat in the living room sprawled out on the sofa watching basketball games, her round belly hanging out of her sweatshirt and her aching feet up on the coffee table. Every time I showed up, she would turn and say, "Y'all want some dinner?" Kathryn's barbecued spare ribs melted right off the bone and into your mouth, and her crispy, moist fried chicken surpassed any I had ever tasted. Green vegetables like broccoli or spinach were cooked till they were mushy and brown and her potatoes were drowned in cream and butter. I tried to avoid butter and fried foods, but whenever Kathryn offered any to me, I quickly grabbed a fork and bib.

She was able to fix Susan up with nails so long they could hold a house together. We pounded and pounded and finally had the branch and its birds secured and settled in with Mama.

Cypress Manor had accepted Mama in spite of her growing immobility. The pain was still intense, so a rheumatoid specialist tried another form of painkiller, the Duragesic patch. This medication flipped her out and she grew so paranoid from it that she thought I was part of a conspiracy and called 911! The specialist that prescribed it took no responsibility and said to me, "Well, what do you expect me to do? It's 5:00 on Friday. Call the office on

Monday or take her to the emergency room."

Needless to say, we never saw that doctor again.

I discussed the situation with Mama's regular internist and he prescribed a nasal spray for pain called Miacalcin. The results were horrific. Her hallucinations were so intense that she got up, fell down, and lay screaming in her room in the middle of the day for twenty minutes. She had broken her arm and nobody heard her or came to her rescue. Fortunately my niece Christine, who lived an hour away, happened to come by for a visit, found Mama, and dialed 911. Then she called me.

"Auntie Bethie, Grandma is lying on the floor."

"What? Is she conscious? Did you call 911? Is there any staff member there?"

"I called 911 but Grandma is talking really weird. She said that the door flew off the hinges and knocked her down."

I heard the sirens in the background. "I'm on my way." Since I lived so close I arrived just as they were loading Mama into the ambulance.

"Is she okay? Is anything broken?" I rushed to Mama's side, whose eyes seemed a little glazed over.

"Mama! What happened?" She recognized me and said, "The door just flew off the hinges and knocked me down." I looked up at the medical technician for answers.

"She has a broken arm and it looks like she is coming off hallucinations. Is she on any medicine?" I told him about the nasal spray.

Mama's internist wasn't on staff at our hospital, so when

we got to the emergency room, Dr. Hart handled her case. I guess the older I get the younger the doctors seem, because he looked like he was twelve. He was young, athletic, handsome, and a snazzy dresser. His curly brown hair and dreamy dark eyes made Mama feel better right away. She could be quite coquettish at times. And I liked him because he actually listened to me when I discussed her history and pain treatment. I think he was impressed because I was knowledgeable about most drugs that Mama had taken and the direct effect they had on her. I also questioned his ideas and decisions, and my feeling is that most doctors appreciate that. It's so easy to treat doctors like God and trust and accept any and every decision they make. But they're not God. They're under a lot of pressure and have too many patients. Mama needed an advocate, and it was me. I did my homework and felt strongly about working with her doctor as a team. Dr. Hart was open to that so we got on right away.

Poor Mama was still on at least eighteen meds a day at that point, and the cost was over $600 per month with no insurance coverage. Before she underwent surgery for her arm, Dr. Hart and I decided the best thing to do was to start over. We sat down and went through every pill. Turns out she was taking pills that were of no use to her at that stage of her arthritis. No more patches, sprays and intense narcotics. Dr. Hart took her off long-term painkillers and prescribed a short-term painkiller to be used more frequently. It worked out great. With changes in her medication, Mama came back. Her pain was somewhat managed, she was in her head again, and within days she was herself. Plus she had a new doctor that both of us liked and respected.

With her meds sorted out, it was time to schedule her arm surgery. I was terrified of Mama undergoing surgery at eighty-eight, especially with such brittle bones, but her broken arm required it. Her surgeon was another young and attractive doctor with a killer smile that melted Mama. When she saw him, her arm almost healed itself.

In the pre-op room I asked her if she was scared, and her answer was predictable. She looked up at her doctor, reached for his hand, and replied, "No, not with Dr. Billings doing the surgery."

During Mama's surgery, my sister Susan and I waited together at the hospital.

"I'm not taking Mama back to Cypress Manor to live." Susan looked at me, surprised. "What! Really?"

"Really. For what we're paying, a staff member should have been there. There is no excuse for what happened."

She looked interested. "So, what are you gonna do? The price is right there. What if we have to spend more money? Where are we going to find another place that reasonable?"

"I don't care. I refuse to put her through anything like that again. We'll sell her house if we have to."

Susan saw the light. "I agree. Maybe we could find a prettier place with a better staff."

I nodded yes. "That idiot doctor told me she was not safe with me, but this never would have happened on my watch. I mean, I know she can't come home again, and that alone is awful; but if she can't be in her own home then I will find the best place in town. I don't care if I have to rob a bank." Susan agreed and I added, "Too bad I'm so old. I would become a hooker, but at my age I would have to pay them."

The decision was made and Susan was in full support. "She has to be at Westland House for rehab for several weeks, so that will give us time to move her out and into a new place." We high-fived each other.

"Let's say a prayer that the perfect place manifests." We crossed ourselves and prayed to the Blessed Mother and my Blessed Shary. A nurse came in and told us that we could see Mama. Fearfully, Susan and I followed the nurse, our arms draped around each other, hoping that Mama was okay. We found a miraculous surprise. Mama came out of the operating room, grinning. Her big blue eyes were clear and her cheeks were rosy. Dr. Billings was holding her hand and said, "She did great." He patted her forehead and bid her goodbye. She was amazingly lucid.

Susan and I were on either side of her. "How do you feel Mama?"

"Oh, I'm fine dears, how are you? You must be exhausted. Why don't you go home now? I'll be fine." We walked with the orderly to her room and stayed until she fell asleep.

Susan and I kissed her and I said, "Sleep with the angels, Mama. We love you." Mama never felt any pain or discomfort from the surgery.

I looked at Susan and tears were in her eyes. I hugged her and said, "Mama is okay. After they transfer her to rehab tomorrow, we'll find her the best place in town. Right now, let's have a drink."

Susan and I visited a very happy Mama every day at Westland House. The staff was cheerful, personable, and compassionate, and the food was fabulous. They prepared very fresh grilled fish or chicken with green veggies, wonderful crisp salads and her favorite: fabulous desserts. Westland House is set in a spectacular forest. Deer, bunnies, and raccoons appeared at her sliding glass door, and birds were constantly singing. It was such a Disney setting that I expected Snow White to show up any minute with seven little people and a hot apple pie.

Shary Farr, the angel in street clothes, suggested a beautiful assisted-living home, Country Oak Inn. It was close by and had a huge light and airy bedroom, and plenty of wall space for Mama's paintings and the damn branch. There was also enough room for her favorite furniture from home, including her television, stereo, and various ceramic, porcelain, and wooden angels. Outside her large window were wonderful old gnarled oak trees and tall pines that towered over an emerald green lawn. There were only six residents in this renovated home, along with an entertaining miniature poodle named "Muffin." All kinds of birds chirped throughout the day and roosted in the oak at night.

Our cars were packed for Country Oak Inn and the branch was the last to be stowed. Susan and I were so exhausted from moving all of Mama's belongings that we just threw the branch in the back seat. We lost a few more twigs here and there along the way, but the birds survived the trip relatively unscathed.

Once again, we found a perfect spot for the damn branch. After several attempts, the branch was finally secured. It looked adorable and we knew it would please Mama.

Mama wanted to live at Westland House forever, so we had to have a nurse gently tell her when it was time to be discharged. It cushioned the blow when we told her that she was NOT going back to Cypress Manor, and that Susan and I had already moved her into Country Oak Inn. She was apprehensive but trusted us. And at the cost of $5,000 a month, we had no choice but to sell her house.

When Susan and I wheeled Mama into her new home, she instantly loved it. Muffin welcomed her with wet kisses, and I put on one of her favorite CDs, Sarah Brightman. And of course it warmed her heart that we had remembered to hang her beloved branch.

We'd bought new sheets and a coverlet so Mama's bed would look like a garden of violets. The house in Michigan where we grew up had a wonderful mulberry tree in the backyard. We called it the "umbrella tree" because the twiggy branches bent to the ground like a willow and it looked like a giant umbrella. Every May hundreds of purple, lavender, and white violets blanketed the ground under the tree. We picked handfuls, put them in tiny vases, and placed them in front of statues of the Virgin Mary because May was the month of The Blessed Mother.

Unfortunately, we quickly became disillusioned with

Country Oak Inn, and I started having my doubts about the owner, Charlene. Only one staff member spoke English, and I had a feeling the workers were paid below minimum wage. The food was usually frozen lasagna or five-for-a-dollar enchiladas that Mama had trouble eating because her teeth were old and sensitive. I asked Charlene to please make sure the staff served Mama soft foods. Meat was hard for her to chew and impossible for her to cut up with her crippled little hands. Often when I dropped by at dinnertime, I found Mama sitting in her chair looking at her cold food that nobody had cut up for her, the meat so tough that even Muffin couldn't chew it.

At Country Oak there was an elderly resident named Ernie, whose room was at the opposite end of the house from Mama's. He was a large man with grey hair and a pleasant face; and in spite of his Alzheimer's, he seemed happy. Ernie was a wanderer and talked incessantly using his hands. Often when I was in the office with Charlene or in Mama's room, Ernie would wander in chatting away, and then take a seat. Everybody accepted him and let him hang around because he was harmless and never showed signs of anger.

All the doors at Country Oak Inn that opened to the outside had alarms so the staff could hear if a resident left the building. These alarms actually spoke, "The door is open. The door is shut." Sometimes Ernie would spend his afternoons opening a door and then shutting it, over and over again. Luckily I couldn't hear it from Mama's room when her own door was closed, but when I opened her door I heard, "THE DOOR IS OPEN. THE DOOR IS SHUT.

THE DOOR IS OPEN. THE DOOR IS SHUT."

Ernie was finally banned from visiting Mama's room after he walked in yakking, sat on one of her chairs, peed, then left. As shocking as it was, it was sort of amusing—and fortunately, the wet cushion belonged to Charlene, not Mama.

One evening after work I decided to surprise Mama with prawns and salad from her favorite seafood restaurant. When I entered her room, I was suddenly aware of how tiny she looked in her oversized lift chair.

"Oh darling I am so happy to see you," she said, reaching out to me with her frail little arms.

I knelt down and hugged her as her tears fell on my neck. She held me as tight as she could, considering she had no strength. I found her boney little hand under her pink shawl and held it.

"What's wrong Mama? Are you in more pain than usual?" I looked into her soul and felt her pain. It was, after all, quite obvious.

"I'm sorry dear. I dreamt that I was back at the A-frame sitting by the pond painting. I hated to wake up. I miss painting so much. If only there was some way I could hold a brush; some way I could walk again." Then she sobbed as I held her tighter.

"Oh Mama, I am so sorry. You don't deserve this."

"I don't mean to burden you with this. I never wanted to be a burden to my children. I just don't want to live anymore. I go from my chair to my bed. What kind of life is this? I just wanna die."

"Oh Mama, I feel so helpless that I can't make it all go away like you did when we were kids. Maybe there is a possibility that you can walk. I'll call Dr. Hart in the morning and see if we can get a physical therapist to come evaluate you." I looked up at one of her angels on the wall and prayed for guidance. There were no words to console Mama.

Suddenly Muffin came bounding into the room as if I called her, jumped on Mama's lap, and enthusiastically licked her tears. In the process, she tore open a wound on Mama's arm, but it was a small price to pay for Muffin's perfect timing.

Weeks later Charlene moved a piano into the living room and I asked, "So what's the piano for? Are you storing it for someone, or are we having a concert?"

Charlene was excited. "We're getting a new resident. He's played piano at several piano bars in town."

"Why is he moving in? Is he sick?"

"He is getting forgetful and needs to be watched, but he can walk and bathe himself. He will be here tomorrow. They call him E.J."

The next day was Mother's Day, and E.J. moved in and was scheduled to perform. Mama wasn't big on social functions because she couldn't hold a glass or fork and it was hard for her to hear. (I had taken her to a hearing specialist and had her fitted for little hearing aids but they buzzed all the time and were too hard to put in.) In spite of Mama's arguments, Susan, our other sister Janet, and I dolled her up and wheeled her into the living room. E.J. was seated at the piano and playing "Strangers in the Night." He was a good-looking elderly man in his eighties, and he wore a beautiful royal blue sweater that matched his eyes. His daughters, Wendy and Jane, were singing along so we joined in the "dooby dooby doos." When the song ended, E.J. asked for requests. Much to our astonishment, Mama yelled out, "Mack the Knife!" We pushed her wheelchair close to the piano so she could hear better, and it was love at first sight. Mama looked beautiful. When the concert was over, E.J., Jane, and Wendy and her husband Max, joined us in Mama's room. We drank wine and ate cheese and crackers, and had a great time. E.J. told corny jokes that made us roll our eyes and laugh—and made Mama glow.

From that day on, when we visited Mama, E.J. was in her room and she was beaming. Once when I arrived, her door was shut. Concerned that the staff was in there and something tragic had happened, I knocked, and then entered. I saw E.J. trying to get up off his knees at Mama's feet, and Mama struggling to button her blouse.

"Can I get those buttons for you, Mama?" I enjoyed that. She grinned a sheepish grin.

"Oh thank you, dear."

With a red face and huge smile, E.J. slicked his very messy brown and gray hair back. To this day, I am not sure exactly how far they went, but I think body parts were caressed. I told E.J. he could have fun with Mama as long as he didn't "knock her up." He and Mama laughed at that for days.

Everybody was excited that Mama had a fun, loving

man who wanted to hang out with her. Like Dad, E.J. loved jokes and told them constantly. Problem was, he was in the beginning stage of dementia so he told the same jokes over and over—but it didn't matter because Mama was happy. Sometimes we put her in her wheelchair and took her around the neighborhood, always accompanied by E.J. and Muffin. Occasionally, we took Mama and E.J. down the coast to a restaurant that overlooked the Pacific Ocean. We ordered Mama's favorite nachos and drinks, then we watched for whale spouts in the distance. E.J. gave Mama a reason to get up in the morning and put on her hot pink lipstick. We considered moving his bed next to hers, but we were afraid that he might roll over and crush her.

One morning the phone rang while I was still in a deep sleep, and I answered it only half awake. "Helloooo." It was Mama.

"Hi darling, are you still sleeping?" I abruptly awoke, concerned that something had happened.

"Mama? Are you okay? What's wrong?" I could feel her smile over the phone.

"'Oh I'm fine, dear but I have a favor to ask you." I grabbed the clock and squinted to see the time while pushing my hair out of my face and wiping the drool off my chin. It was 7:00 a.m. "What do you need Mama? Is everything okay?" I was still quite dozy, although my cats, Incha and Toes, were up at this point and walking on top of me.

"Well, E.J. was hoping you could go to the drug store and get some Viagra."

I was awake now.

"What? Are you kidding me? First of all, a doctor has to prescribe it, and second of all, I think E.J. may be on medications already that may not mix well with Viagra."

There was disappointment in her voice. "Oh really? I guess that could be true."

Amused, I answered, "God, Mama, I really wish I could help you guys out, but E.J. has to check with his physician first. I mean, I would happy to get it, but Viagra is not an over-the-counter drug. Sorry, Mama."

"Oh, okay. You're probably right dear. Can you get back to sleep? I won't bother you any more."

"Mama, you know you can call me any time for anything. I'm just sorry that I can't help. I will come up and see you later. I love you."

"I love you, too, darling. I'm glad you're coming to visit later."

A few blissful months went by then sadly it was discovered that E.J. had stage-four pancreatic cancer. His daughter Wendy didn't think much of Charlene either, and insisted on taking E.J. home to live with her and her husband. This broke our hearts, but we arranged play dates; and either we took Mama over to their house or Wendy brought him back over to Country Oak Inn so they could spend time together. E.J. soon became very ill and then slipped into a coma. Mama was melancholy and asked Susan and I if we would take her over to say good-bye. We left her alone by his side for a while, and then we entered the room and lifted her up so she could get close. Mama's tears were trickling down E.J.'s face as she kissed him good-bye for the last time. E.J. died the next day. Gifts he had given Mama like Valentine hearts, stuffed bears, flowers, and cards became invaluable treasures that she even slept with. Wendy presented Mama with the royal blue sweater he was wearing when they met, and occasionally Mama asked us to put it on her.

Mama was frustrated that she could no longer walk on her own. She had been getting physical therapy, however, and was determined to try. The problem was that nobody on the staff would practice with her or help her with her exercises, so her frustration grew. The staff was too lazy to lift her up and put her on a commode or wheel her into the bathroom. Then Charlene insisted we buy diapers for her. The maddening part was that Mama wasn't incontinent. Poor thing. How humiliating.

I decided that if Mama had a power chair, she could get a little more mobility and maybe visit the living room occasionally. It might cheer her up and give her some sense of independence. I called a company from an advertisement I had seen on television and described her situation, gave them her weight, and let them choose which chair was appropriate for her.

The shiny new green power chair arrived. The instructor took it out of the box, set it up, and gave us a lesson. An hour later when he left, we decided to take Mama for a practice spin around the neighborhood. Mama forgot everything he had taught her. I walked beside her to guide her along, but she had a tendency to veer into the traffic, so I found myself yelling, "To the right, to the right, TO THE RIGHT!!

STOP, MAMA, STOP!" I reached down to steer it myself but I ran over my own foot, so we headed back. Once in the house, Mama took the paint off the front door, left a huge black scrape on the white wall in the hallway, and almost took the door off as she entered her room. All Mama had to do was to let go of the joystick and the chair would stop, but she didn't get it. Once in her room, she rammed a chair that rammed a console that her huge TV sat on. But she didn't stop. She kept right on going and rammed the console into another chair that rammed into a little round table that rammed into the wall. So before Mama destroyed the entire house, I returned the chair. To this day, the image of little Mama driving that huge green power chair with a smile on her face and her white hair blowing back from the speed is a sight forever embedded in my memory and still makes me chuckle.

I grew to dislike Charlene and not trust her. I went so far as to call Ombudsman and even the state to file complaints. The state had already received several against her, including one from Wendy, E.J.'s daughter. Soon the state shut down Country Oak Inn, and we were left to find another assisted living facility that would take Mama in spite of her immobility. I was determined not to put her in a skilled nursing home no matter what the cost.

We discovered Lupine Meadows. It was a little farther away from Susan and me but seemed quite pleasant and very peaceful, with only five residents. Mama's room was much smaller but very light, and had a sliding glass door onto a cute, sunny little patio. Susan and I flew into action and bought colorful potted flowers, a variety of bird feeders, including one for hummingbirds, and a birdbath. We placed a sweet-faced stone angel so it looked at Mama through the window and watched over her. We had to store most of her furniture because there was very little space.

After we had everything out of Mama's room at Country Oak Inn, Susan and I looked at each other, sighed deeply, and said in unison, "Oh hell—the damn branch." We lost another half dozen twigs on this trip to Lupine Meadows, and a couple of birds fell off. We managed to recover the birds, but finding wall space was almost impossible. Finally, we chose a spot above the T.V. within Mama's view, and once again we went through hell trying to secure it. It brought Mama such joy that we never let on what a pain in the ass that damn branch had become. Mama sat amused as she watched me go through all sorts of contortions trying to hold the branch in place while Susan pounded in too many very long nails. Once secured, Susan and I high-fived and I said, "You know, Sis, I think we've earned us a couple of cocktails. What do you say we meander across the street and knock back one or two?"

Susan, always up for fun, said, "I'm in!"

Just then, a caregiver appeared with Mama's dinner, her first at Lupine Meadows. The food didn't look fabulous, but anything was better than Country Oak Inn's five-for-a-dollar frozen enchiladas. Mary was Tonganese, and she was wonderful and gentle with Mama. She wrapped a bib around Mama's neck as Mama encouraged us, "You girls go and have a drink. I'm in good hands." She looked up at

Mary, with a confident smile.

Mary gave us a reassuring look and gently touched Mama's shoulder; then smiled, nodded, and said, "She'll be fine."

I handed Mary a box of Clouds for Mama, the chocolate-covered caramel and pecan candies from Trader Joe's that are like turtles. Mama adored them. Whenever Susan or I went to Trader Joe's we always asked each other, "How many boxes of Clouds did you get for Mama?" Five or six was the normal response.

"If you give her one of these after dinner and before you brush her teeth," we told Mary, "she will love you forever."

Mama, able to spot a box of Clouds from across a room, lit up. "Thank you, darlings."

"We'll be back in a little while to say good night." We walked across the street to a wonderful old hotel and sat at the bar. Susan had her Old Fashioned and I had my mandarin orange vodka and soda. Susan raised her glass. "Here's to Mama."

I raised my glass, "And here's to the damn branch." We clinked glasses and downed our drinks; then with nice little buzzes, we headed back to Mama's to wish her sweet dreams.

As it turned out, Lupine Meadows should never have accepted Mama. She was the size of Tinker Bell, so she hardly weighed anything, but the caregivers were too old to lift her. I explained that there was a technique to lifting her but they never paid attention and only complained.

And Mama herself wasn't happy there, so we tried

everything to make up for it. We rented two of her favorite concerts on DVD: Celtic Woman and Nigel Kennedy. I purchased her favorite PBS movie of all time, *Pride and Prejudice* with Colin Firth. Mama adored Colin Firth, so we hung his photographs everywhere. But it was a boring existence for her there at Lupine Meadows. It was on a busy street with no sidewalk, so we couldn't wheel her around to give her a change of scenery. And there were no pets to make a fuss over her. It was affecting all of us.

Then our biggest fear materialized. Mama developed bedsores on the backs of her heels, because the caregivers rarely got her up. If they did get her up it was only to transfer her to the lift chair where her heels still touched the panel that could be raised up. This had occurred ten years earlier, when Dad was taking care of her. She went through months and months of agonizing debridement and painful whirlpool baths in physical therapy. It took a good year for bedsores to heal, but they finally did. In spite of our insistence that pillows be kept under Mama's calves so her heels wouldn't touch the bed or the chair, nobody listened or took our concerns and suggestions seriously.

Visiting Nurses came regularly for a week or so. Then they dropped the ball. I called the doctor, who in turn called them. Soon the sores had advanced to stage four and were infected down to the bone. The doctor had no choice but to admit Mama to the hospital. As much as I chastised the nursing organization responsible, they blew me off. I should have gone to the state, but my main concern was Mama. She was so brave and rarely complained.

I was aghast that the hospital wanted to release Mama after only two days. If that wasn't bad enough, Dr. Hart insisted that she go to into a skilled nursing home to continue therapy and not back to Lupine Meadows or any assisted living facility. I couldn't understand why she couldn't be admitted to Westland House for treatment and therapy, but it was out of the question. I was so upset that I really didn't know what to do. The grim reality of putting Mama in a skilled nursing home had arrived. When I think of such places, I picture the asylum in *One Flew Over the Cuckoo's Nest:* huge, impersonal, cold, noisy, and ugly. I'd seen *Dateline* and *20/20* documentaries on the horror and abuse that can go on in those places. And I was being told to put my beloved Mama—my best friend—in one?

The facilities we looked at were so dismal and depressing that I just couldn't do it. I couldn't place Mama in any of them, save one: Pine Hills. Of course, there was a waiting list. I begged, bribed, yelled, and did whatever it took to get Mama into that place, but to no avail. I looked the discharge nurse in the eye, touched her arm, led her into her office, shut the door, and said to her, "There must be a way to get my Mama into Westland House rehab at least for a couple of days or until a bed opens up at Pine Hills."

She just stared at me and said, "I am so sorry, but Westland House is not an option and I can't make a bed open up at Pine Hills. I have no choice."

I was not going to be defeated. I was close to hysteria and she continued to glare at me.

"There is nothing I can do. Now I have other patients

I must attend to." She started to leave and I moved between her and the door.

"Look, imagine this is your mother. She is lucid and knows exactly what is going on. She was a talented and successful artist until a disease crippled her so that she is almost bedbound. Now she has to go into a place where she may have two roommates that are either moaning out of their heads or sick from meds or chemo. Would you want your mother to live like that?"

She showed a human side. "I am so sorry but I can't manifest a bed there. You'll just have to find another facility, and you better hurry because here comes the gurney to transfer her." I looked outside the door to see two orderlies entering Mama's room.

"Where do they think they are taking her? We haven't made any arrangements with any place yet."

The cold stare returned. "They will take her to the nearest place that has an opening and we will make the arrangements."

I flew to Mama's side. "NO! You aren't taking her anywhere right now." I had no clue what I was going to say next and just prayed for divine intervention. Suddenly the phone rang in the discharge nurse's office. I stayed close to Mama and took her hand. Then the nurse came in with a look on her face like she had just seen God and announced, "Pine Hills has a bed." Mama was discharged.

There were ninety residents in Pine Hills, which was a huge, cheerless institution. We fought to get Mama into a bright room with a bed next to a sliding glass door that looked out into the forest. With my constant nagging, it happened; the admissions officer was able to move Mama into one shortly after her arrival there. We brought her birdbath, her bird feeders, and her potted flowers that were still blooming. We cheered up her tiny environment as best we could. It was close to Christmas, so we put tiny colored lights around her mirror and a little evergreen tree decked with tiny clear lights and birds outside her door. The "damn branch" barely survived this trip and there was only one possible place to hang it where Mama could see it. I had to pile phone books and stools on top of a cold, metal chest of drawers so I could reach the spot. We bent some of the little branches because the only place we could hang it was so high that part of it brushed against the ceiling, but we had no other options. Everyday we had to flip one of the little birds right side up after it fell over. The branch was beginning to look a little tired and sparse, but there were still plenty of little limbs left for us to break off in the future. The branch continued to bring joy to Mama so it was well worth our efforts.

Mama had a screamer for a roommate. This poor woman, Rose, lay in bed yelling, "Help me! Help me!" all day and into the night. Her family rarely visited her, so sometimes Susan or I went over to her and held her hand, kissed her forehead, talked to her, or helped her with her blankets.

"Does Rose keep you up at night Mama?"

Mama smiled and replied, "Well, dear, that's the one good thing about being hard of hearing. It doesn't bother me much at all." So Mama was able to sleep through poor Rose's fears.

Pine Hills took Mama for physical therapy regularly. Dr. Hart looked in on her once a week, and within three months the bedsores were completely healed. The only requirement was to keep a pillow under her calves so the sores wouldn't return. Susan made signs that stated, "HEELS MUST STAY OFF THE BED. PILLOWS UNDER HER CALVES AT ALL TIMES," and placed them all over the room.

Mama was still not incontinent, but instead of taking her in the wheelchair to the toilet, they diapered her up and occasionally she sat there for hours waiting for a change.

Soon Mama complained that her heel hurt. We looked, and there it was, one of the evil fiery dragons had returned with a fury. The sore was about the size of a quarter in diameter, inflamed, swollen, and oozing. I didn't even take time to push the call button. I ran past the nurses' station and burst open the door to the head nurse's office.

"What the hell is going on here? Have you even looked at my Mom's heels in a week?"

I startled the nurse, who was on the phone. She hung up and asked, "What's the problem?"

"WHAT'S THE PROBLEM??? When is the last time you looked at Mom's heels?? What is wrong with you people?" I darted out the door and headed towards the owner's office. I threw open his door but nobody was there. I went to the front desk.

"Where is he?" I demanded. A young receptionist looked up at me.

"I think he is playing golf." I looked up towards heaven and back to her.

"Well get him on his cell phone and tell him to get his ass off the golf course and get here ASAP, or I will have the state agents here so fast . . ." The head nurse saw me and came over, but before she could speak I turned to her.

"What kind of place is this?? My Mom comes in with bedsores which you healed nicely, and then two months later not only have they come back, but now one of them is bigger than ever!"

She touched my shoulder and gently pushed me in the direction of Mama's room. "I am so sorry. Let's go see her." Both of us entered Mama's room and the nurse immediately looked at the sores.

My blood pressure skyrocketed. "Well, what do you have to say? How could you let this happen?"

She took a close look at both of them. "I am so sorry. I am going to call the wound specialist right now. Don't worry, we're on it."

I wasn't finished with her yet. "You are NOT 'on it.' You screwed up big time and you are not doing your job."

Susan was with me and spoke up. "I have signs posted all over this room that state to keep her heels off the bed and a pillow under her calves. What do we have to do? Move in?"

No matter how much I yelled and pointed fingers, it wasn't going to heal the sores any faster. Mama was the least upset of anybody and her energy calmed me down when the owner of the nursing home arrived with the wound specialist.

That night, I lay awake crying, upset and helpless. Then, able to recognize a miracle, I was struck with an awesome idea. Six months ago I had moved out to the country in Carmel Valley, about ten miles inland from Carmel. I loved it out there because it was warmer. I had hoped to find a cozy little farmhouse but instead I found a 1700-square-foot hi-tech palace that was nothing like I had imagined or wanted. It was not my style at all. I had no intention of renting it, but the landlady had made me an offer I couldn't refuse. She liked me because I told her I was all about caregiving for Mama. Her father had died in her arms nine months prior, so she was sympathetic and kept lowering the rent until I couldn't resist.

A huge plus was that it was just up the hill from Susan's house so we could walk to each other's place. My house looked like a huge cardboard box with high ceilings and gigantic picture windows that I had no clue how to wash. Light hardwood floors were throughout the entire place except for the warm terra cotta tiles on the kitchen floor. The dining room was next to the kitchen and there was a room beyond the dining room that was a guest room, entertainment center, and office. Off that room was a funky little bathroom with a shower.

Upstairs, the master bedroom was a bright, sunny loft with hardwood floors and at the end of the room were two long, mirrored sliding closet doors. A set of French doors opened to a small wood deck that faced west with a panoramic view of the mountains.

I loved waking up in that bedroom. It was like waking up in a tree house. A giant California redwood tree graced the view outside the window that faced north, and a majestic, twisted old oak tree was to the right of the deck. I heard frogs, crickets, and owls. Many nights I opened the drapes and lay in bed watching the moon come up, stars shoot across the sky, and constellations appear.

Cocktails on the bed at sunset were not uncommon. Friends would come over, and my two cats, Incha and Toes, would join us while we watched the sun disappear behind the mountains. We called it "kitty cocktail hour," and it became quite a popular ritual.

The miraculous part of this house was that the bathroom off the master bedroom was enormous. There was no curtain or door, just a shower and drain. It was perfect for wheelchair accessibility.

CHAPTER 8

Forty-eight hours after I had made a scene at Pine Hills, Mama's room was ready at my house and I was almost prepared. I was happy to move downstairs into the guest room so she could have the easy-access bathroom and the view. Susan and I had an hour to transform my bedroom for Mama before we were to pick her up from that horrible place. Home Health Care finally delivered the bed and airflow mattress. The electric lift chair was picked up and another one delivered. I managed to tidy up the room in spite of what a cluttered mess it had been an hour and a half earlier, including the papers and ninety-eight Tylenol tablets scattered all over the floor. Susan left work early and showed up to help make the bed and tidy up while I organized all those boxes of supplies in closets and cupboards. We did whatever we could think of to make Mama feel welcome, including hanging the "damn branch." Susan and I struggled with it in the car, and it had permanently lost at least one bird along with more twigs, but we managed to secure it on the wall above her bed.

We were finally prepared to bring Mama home. Susan and I were so excited to pick her up from Pine Hills, where she was patiently waiting in her wheelchair for us. I went to the office and picked up a refund check. Then I went to the nurse's station to collect the remaining meds and off we went with Mama.

By the time we got home and settled in, it was dinnertime so we ordered takeout: crab cakes, pasta, and Caesar salad. I filled my glass with vodka and club soda, Susan filled hers with wine, and we filled Mama's sippy cup with sparking apple juice. The cats had Fancy Feast, and we all toasted Mama.

"Here's to you, Mama. You have been through so much and you haven't complained. Your courage is astounding and I am thrilled and honored to have you with me. I hope you will be happy here." She looked so cute and cozy in her new soft white nightie with tiny pink roses. She raised her sippy cup.

"Thank you darlings for all you have done. I just hope I won't be too much of a burden on you." Incha jumped on the bed purring and settled in right next to her.

"We'll make it work. I love you so much, Mama."

"And I love my darling daughters. I don't know how to thank you, dears."

We sipped our drinks, and then ate. After dinner I brought her a welcome-home box of Clouds. She always had room in her belly for a Cloud. While she chewed and cherished each bite of her two Clouds, I hooked up her new stereo system and found her favorite 30s and 40s station.

The huge room was cozy. Her antique Chinese lamps that we dug out of storage glowed, and the soft light complemented her own beautiful paintings that we had hung. With the French doors opening onto the small deck, she would be able to see her favorite flowers that we put in pots of all shapes and sizes just outside. They were the kind of flowers she had painted before the arthritis set into her hands. She loved bright orange California poppies, white Shirley poppies with red tips, iridescent blue and purple delphinium, hot pink and golden ranunculus, and springy yellow, white and lavender freesias. Occasionally she added a hummingbird or butterfly. Mama painted her flowers in their natural environment, as opposed to traditional still lifes. Her work was sensitive, delicate, and beautiful.

After Mama's first dinner at home, Incha and Toes curled up on her bed, and of course she loved that. It was a delightful evening until an embarrassed look came over her sweet little face. She looked up at me and said, "Sorry, dear."

Mama was still not incontinent, but in spite of all the money we had paid, not one person at any of the facilities had taken her to the toilet, so she grew accustomed to going in diapers. Here at my home I would insist the caregivers get her to the bathroom or to the borrowed commode that sometimes served as my chair.

I decided right away that first night that I had to devise a system for this part of the caregiving. I tossed back the remainder of the vodka, went into the bathroom and emerged with the trash basket, wipes, a pail of warm water, under pads, baby powder, a drying towel, a fresh new diaper, and latex gloves.

Susan and I each grabbed a cat much to their dislike, and moved them to her lift chair.

We cleaned her up and it was time to put the new diaper on. The choice was to use a pull-up or the kind with the side tabs. Since we had more with the side tabs and they looked easier to deal with, we chose those. After all, how hard could it be?

Oh my God!!!! We had to do one side at a time, and the hardest part was not having enough diaper on the other side, so every time we thought we had it, one of the tabs tore off. Finally, after wasting half a dozen diapers (and they're not cheap), we managed to secure one. We were so frustrated, and poor Mama had to roll from side to side so she was pretty worn out. It had been a huge day for her.

Mama had been a great sport with no complaints. She held onto her sense of humor, but I knew pain was setting in because it was time for her meds. I wasn't an easy sleeper and I have never been a morning person, so I was apprehensive about this part of the job, but very willing to do it for Mama. She would have done it for me. Hell, she HAD done it for me.

Soon Mama was cozy in her bed with the cats asleep on either side of her, so we hugged and kissed Susan good-bye and settled in for the night. I gently massaged Ponds Moisturizer into Mama's face, applied ChapStick to her lips, and kissed her good night.

"I love you, Mama, and I am so happy you are here with me. Sleep with the angels— and most likely Incha and Toes too."

"Good night, darling, and thank you. I love you too."

My head didn't hit the pillow fast enough and I didn't move until that startling alarm clock went off at 3:45 a.m. I threw on my robe and UGGS, turned on every light in the house to help wake me up, and dragged myself up all fifteen steps. Before I woke Mama, I got her pills and water ready, and then gently touched her hand. Incha had taken on the role of head caregiver and was quite incensed that I disturbed her at all. "Mama," I softly murmured, even though she was snoring like an old bear. I softly rubbed her shoulder, "Mama, it's time for your meds."

She awoke with a smile, and in a slurred voice she said, "Okay, dear."

I remember that moment as if it were today. I felt so full of love, warmth, peace, joy, and gratitude that she was with me. I gave her the pills, then kissed her good night again. I told her I loved her and staggered back down the stairs and into bed. But I didn't fall back to sleep. I worried whether or not the caregiver would show up at 9:00 a.m. sharp, because if she didn't and I slept through the alarm, then Mama would miss that painkiller and she would suffer for hours. I also wondered if the caregiver would help clean and if she cooked.

The next morning Mila showed up at 9:00 a.m., ready to work. She was in her late 60s, and was small, tidy, and in relatively good shape. She spoke with a strong Filipino accent but her English was understandable. She gave Mama her meds right on schedule, and since Mama never ate breakfast, she fell back to sleep. Then Mila cleaned her bedroom and bathroom, took a few notes, and prepared lunch.

I have a small business hand painting chickens on glassware. Unfortunately, my worktable was right next to the kitchen so I was an easy target for Mila's inquisitive mind.

"How many you paint in one day? You can put in dishwasher? How much you get for one? My daughter, she artist."

In spite of Mila's annoying curiosity, she did have a good heart. She brought a special salve from the Philippines to rub on Mama's feet or neck—a thoughtful gesture, I thought, for her first day.

Apparently Mila had been a singer in the Philippines, and she sang along to some of the old songs on Mama's radio station. She had a sweet voice, and I had a feeling that in her heyday she had been a lot of fun. She did have a good sense of humor besides being quite beautiful.

Mila stuck strictly to the rules and schedules that first day. Mama was on a short-term painkiller because her body just couldn't handle anything stronger. She could go off her pain med schedule and take extra if necessary. Later that afternoon I was painting downstairs when I heard Mama moan. That sound pierced right through my heart. I yelled up to Mila. "Mila, is Mama okay?"

"Her neck hurt her pretty badly. I theeenk the arthritis in her neck" Mila replied.

"Then go ahead and give her another pain killer." I went

back to my work.

A few minutes went by and just when I got back in the creative groove, Mama moaned again, but this time it was more of a bone-chilling wail. The hairs on the back of my neck stood straight up. She sounded like a ghost in a classic horror story. Obviously, her pain was extreme and whatever had to be done to stop it had to be done immediately. When she was that bad, I wanted her to know I was close, so I headed upstairs. I sat by her side and stroked her head.

"Hang in there, Mama. The meds should kick in any minute now." Mila threw me a glance and said, "No, not yet. I not give it to her yet."

Man, I threw her a glance right back and halfway shrieked, "What! Didn't you give her the pill?"

She pointed to her watch. "No, not yet time. Five o'clock she get pill."

I was livid. "Mila," my voice raised a few decibels, "I told you to give it to her fifteen minutes ago. I explained to you earlier that it is okay to give her more painkillers if she is in pain. Give her the pill NOW." With that, Mila jumped and gave Mama the pill. I stayed with Mama until her sobbing ceased. I kissed her and told her she would feel better soon and I went back to my *Chickenware*. Before I went downstairs, I said to Mila, "If Mama is ever in that kind of pain, Mila, remember the sooner she gets the pill, the sooner her suffering will ease up. She can have all she wants. It's okay." I showed her the bottle, which stated that a pill could be given every four to six hours and as needed.

"I'm sorry Meeees Bet. It not happen again."

"Okay Mila. Please remember that. I know it's your first day so some things you learn as you go." I headed back downstairs to my art. I calmed down and got back to my work. Just as I touched the brush to the paint the phone rang. I took a deep breath and repeated my mantra, *God get me through this. God get me through this...*

"Hello?"

"Oh hi. My name is Barbara Parks and I am with the visiting nurses. I have orders from Dr. Hart to come evaluate your mother, Ellen Harris."

I was happy to hear from her in spite of my need to work. "Hi Barbara, my name is Beth. I am Ellen's daughter."

"Hi Beth. I would like to see her first thing tomorrow if that is okay with you. I understand that she has bedsores."

We set up a time, I gave her directions, and I picked up my paintbrush. Mama seemed content and pain free now, so all was well until Mila yelled from upstairs.

"Meees Bet. Your Mama want something to eat."

I found myself yelling. "Then come down and get her a snack." I got up and went to the refrigerator and pulled out some cheese and grapes and set them on a plate with some crackers and cookies.

"Mila, I know it's your first day, but in the future please just come down and grab whatever Mama wants."

"Okay. Thank you Meeees Bet."

I was so frustrated that I needed a walk. My road went straight up a hill for a couple of miles and the surroundings were beautiful. I grabbed my iPod, put on the earphones, and entered into another dimension. On these walks I often saw deer, foxes, and sometimes wild turkeys. Every walk was a magical thrill. It took me about forty-five minutes to hike up and back, and the moment I walked in the door, Mila called me.

"Meeeees Bet! I call your neighbor because your Mama fall."

My face went white. "Is she okay?" On my way up, I thought, *Oh please, God, don't let anything be broken. Please, no more pain for her and no more long nights and early mornings in ER.*

Mila's voice broke my train of second-guessing. "She fine because I know I am going to drop her, so I set her on the floor. But I couldn't get her up, so I call your neighbor to help. He was very nice."

I didn't even know how I felt, but I realized that I needed somebody younger and stronger. Mila was scheduled four days a week, so I had to interview and train a new caregiver. That was about the last thing I wanted to have to do. I was already too tired for this.

Fortunately, Mama was in her lift chair and she was absolutely fine. I told Mila that she had done the right thing by setting Mama down and calling Frank. Then I went directly to the phone and called the agency to find somebody to replace Mila, and while it was ringing I put my head face down on my desk. *God get me through this. God get me through this.*

That was just the first day.

CHAPTER 9

I have mentioned the cats several times, and since they are main characters, I feel it important to give you a little background on them.

In my previous apartment in Carmel, Incha had lived upstairs and belonged to my landlady. He was young, feisty, and very affectionate. He's also a handsome cat—orange and white, long and muscular; and he can out-purr any feline on earth. Sometimes when we were in my living room, Incha would appear outside at the base of the French doors. He would stand on his hind feet, put his paws on the lowest windowpane, and meow. We couldn't hear the meow, we only saw his mouth open and shut with his magnificent, thick white whiskers riding up and down as the window fogged up from his breath. He wanted desperately to come in for some loving, but my dog, Scout, wouldn't allow it.

I only interacted with Incha when his owner was away, which ended up being quite often. When I went upstairs to feed him, he would sit on my lap and we would hang out. He was quite a talker and we would chat until Scout beckoned me with his "come home" whine.

The dreaded day came when a very old and sick Scout had to be put down. The veterinarian came to the house. When they carried Scout out the kitchen door wrapped in his favorite red blanket, Incha was on his way down the stairs, which was odd considering the landlady's door at the top was kept closed. I saw Scout's spirit enter Incha's body, as if Incha had said to Scout, "Ok, I'm ready. Jump in." Incha never went back upstairs. He slept where Scout slept, and he waited for me in the same spot where Scout always had. I missed Scout's face and I missed hiking with him, but he was alive and well in Incha. Soon after that, I moved to the country and Incha came with me.

After a few weeks in our new home, I noticed a cat's head pop out of the shrubs. I figured it was a neighbor's cat and perhaps he and Incha could be buddies. Every day he moved in a little closer. One day while I was in the driveway, I saw Incha run into the garden. I called, "Kitty, kitty, kitty," and he bounded back out of the flowers. A couple of feet behind him, a smaller orange and white cat also bounded out, but with a little more caution. He stopped, sat, looked at me, and meowed a funny, high-pitched meow. He continued talking as he gingerly sauntered up to me, and then hesitated. He put his head almost upside down, rolled over on his back, and stretched out. Then I noticed his "thumbs" protruding dramatically and realized he had six toes on each paw.

"Wow. Come here, kitty." He leaped into my arms. I had no clue where "Toes" lived until I heard a young girl call, "Mittens, Mittens, where are you?"

I called back to her, "Are you calling an orange and white cat with six toes? Does he belong to you, because he's hanging out here. I'll get him for you." I picked up "Mittens" and handed him over the fence. He was back in my yard within an hour. A few days later, those neighbors moved away, leaving "Mittens" behind. I decided then that Mittens was my cat and his new name would be "Toes."

Toes was younger than Incha and soon behaved like an irritating little brother. They would start around 3:00 a.m., when I could hear them leap onto the living room furniture. Claws dug into the overstuffed chairs, area rugs scattered all over the place, and my wooden statue of poor St. Francis was constantly knocked to the floor. Then I heard those eerie, loud, annoying catfight yowls. They growled, hissed, and chased each other upstairs, then downstairs. The pounding of paws was exaggerated on the wooden floors. Tudump, tudump, tudump... up the stairs, tudump, tudump, tudump... down the stairs. One night I suddenly flew out of bed, turned on the lights, and screamed, "I HAVE HAD ENOUGH!" I yelled just as Toes took a flying jump from the couch to the chair. He clung to the side of the chair with his twelve front claws extended while the rest of his body swayed from side to side. His head turned and he looked at me as if he was saying, "What? We're not doing nothing." Flying fur was slowly drifting toward the floor like feathers. Incha, eyes black and wide, stood frozen in his pounce position. They were terrorists by night but by morning they slept like bookends at the foot of my bed, looking like angels.

CHAPTER 10

Sundays were my day with Mama. It gave us a break from the caregivers, plus it saved money. I slept better knowing that I didn't have to worry whether or not the caregiver would show up on time. It was astonishing how stressful having hired helpers was.

Our first Sunday together, I gently woke Mama at 9:00 a.m. and gave her meds, then both of us, along with the cats, fell back to sleep. Around eleven, I made a beautiful, healthy, hearty brunch: a frittata with mushrooms, asparagus, potatoes, and cheese. Then I cut up a honeydew melon and covered it with fresh raspberries from Susan's garden. Mama had herb tea in her sippy cup, and I brewed strong coffee for myself. I went outside and picked some nasturtiums. They were prolific in the garden and produced various shades of orange and yellow, and some were even striped with both colors. I made them into a small bouquet, and put it in a little turquoise vase. I lined Mama's tray with a colorful Guatemalan placemat, set the bouquet and her brunch on it, and headed upstairs before she woke up from her morning nap.

I opened the drapes and looked out over the mountains to greet the day. The birds on the deck scattered, but when I filled their feeder and birdbath, they returned with their friends. There were black-headed juncos, cute little brown sparrows, very vocal chickadees with a white stripe across the side of their face, Steller's jays, and towhees. There was also one lone huge gray squirrel with a luxuriant tail. Most majestic of all was a gorgeous, shiny huge black crow we named Russell. He sat on the edge of the birdbath, drank a little, and then flew off with fruit from the expensive designer bird food mixture. Below the ledge where the critters fed were the bright, bountiful pots of flowers, completing a perfect day against the intense blue sky.

With the drapes open, the cats woke up, stretched, yawned, turned, and faced outdoors; then chatted to the birds. It was very serene until Toes got that look in his eye and pounced on Incha, going for the jugular, which then led to a morning cat battle. They yowled and hissed, with their ears as flat as they could be. Then they pounced on Mama's bed, waking her out of a deep sleep. She was quite amused when fur flew all around the room. Claws were extended and deep growls rose from their bellies. In a flash, Toes chased Incha all the way down the stairs and out the door. They were up for the day! I turned on the radio and Louis Armstrong was singing "What a Wonderful World" as I sat Mama up.

"Time for breakfast!" I pulled her tray close and cranked

up the head of her bed so she could see outdoors. I brought up my tray too, so she didn't have to eat alone, and I fed her while I chewed.

"Did you sleep well, darling?" she asked, as always.

"Oh, not bad. I was able to get back to sleep after the 4:00 a.m. because I knew I didn't have to worry about a caregiver." I gathered some berries on a spoon. "How 'bout you?"

She nodded yes, and then asked, "Are you going to paint chickens today?"

I shook my head no and fed her the berries. Mama was a great eater and enjoyed her cuisine. "Naw, I want to hang out with you. I was thinking I would give you a shower."

She smiled. "Oh that would be lovely. But can you manage me?"

"Sure I can. We'll make it fun."

After breakfast I turned the little space heater on in the bathroom, threw some bath towels in a hot dryer, and got Mama out of bed for her shower. Slowly I sat her up in bed and turned her so she could put her feet on the floor. Then I pulled the wheelchair close to the bed, double-checked that the brake was on, and spread some pads on the chair. I braced one foot between her legs and counted one, two, three; lifted her up, pivoted her around and made sure her bottom was as far back as I could get it; and finally eased her down. Of course, I wasn't always able to "ease" her down—sometimes she plopped down, and when I was really exhausted I occasionally plopped down on top of her. It made us laugh. Then off to the warm bathroom we went, and I wheeled her into the huge shower stall. I lifted her onto a special shower chair. Mama loved freesia-smelling shower gels and soap, so I lathered her up, and when she was squeaky clean I took the towels out of the dryer and bundled her up like a newborn. That was her favorite part. She looked so pink and so cute.

I laid pads on the wheelchair, then strategically placed her diaper so she would land right in the middle, because if she didn't, then she would sit on a sticky tab and it would be tough to get it off. I sprinkled baby powder on the diaper (but as days went by and my patience grew thinner, I sometimes squeezed the baby powder so hard, a big cloud of dust rose up and made both of us cough). Once I had her back in the wheelchair, I wheeled her to the bedroom so she could watch the birds while I dressed her.

She sat stark naked while I knelt in front of her trying to secure her diaper. I held one tab in one hand and the other tab in the other hand, so my hands were full. Mama held her sippy cup, but because her hands were twisted and weak from the arthritis, she couldn't hold it any longer. I felt water drip on me and she yelled for me to take the cup. Not wanting to let go of the tab, I quickly grabbed the cup, lifted up her breast, stuck the sippy cup under it, and placed it back down. The cup stayed in place perfectly. From that day on, we stored all sorts of things there: combs, lipstick, rouge, and tissue. Amazing how that extra storage came in handy.

Dressing Mama was enjoyable because she appreciated pretty clothes. Back in the 60s she dressed like Jackie Kennedy in gorgeous, sexy, silk cocktail dresses and Coco Chanel suits with tight skirts and short fitted jackets. Mama had one royal blue suit that I will never forget. It had black fur around the collar and cuffs. The entire outfit was complete with four-inch black stilettos and a black pillbox hat. She looked fabulous. In the 70s, however, the artist in her emerged and she dressed in classy, artsy, bright, splashy print clothes with contemporary handcrafted jewelry. Mama had a flair for style, plus she had the figure for it. I knew how important it was for her to look her best, so I tried to honor that. I continued working in a clothing shop in downtown Carmel two days a week, and the owner was kind enough to let me special-order skirts and tops at cost. Mama could wear turquoise and royal blue, dusty rose and reds, lavenders and purples, periwinkles, and peach; almost any color complimented her curly white hair, baby blue eyes and rosy cheeks. I adorned her with her favorite silver circle necklace, curled her hair, filed her nails, rouged her cheeks and put hot pink lipstick on her lips. She looked gorgeous and still pretty sexy for an eighty-nine-year-old. It was kind of like having a Barbie Doll—only it was more like, disabled–arthritic–overmedicated–confined-to-a-wheelchair Barbie. Hmm. I wonder when Mattel will think of that?

I found myself getting lonely for my friends and wishing they would stop by on Sundays. Once Mama's meds kicked in, she felt good and looked great. And since both of us were rested and not stressed out by caregivers, it was a perfect time for visitors.

My wish came true and friends started coming by. Plasha and Randy were my very close friends of the younger generation and had a little boy, Hayden, whom I adored. Plasha and Randy had always been there for me. They helped me move from house to house, they pitched in when I held garage sales, and they were more than happy to help with some of Mama's needs. They were family and still are. They always brought champagne and orange juice for mimosas, so these Sundays became "Mimosa Sundays."

The house was perfect for kids to run around in, and I provided toys, books, a rocking horse, and DVDs. They loved running up and down the stairs yelling and screaming, which echoed throughout the entire neighborhood. Luckily, Mama was a little deaf, so it didn't disturb her. Hayden was two years old and often went up to visit Mama. His favorite amusement was to grab the control to Mama's electric lift chair, and with the push of a button, he could watch Grandma go up and Grandma go down, and Grandma go up and Grandma go down. Mama just went with the flow, smiling, sometimes with a sippy cup at her mouth. She had a great sense of humor and thoroughly enjoyed Hayden.

When the champagne and orange juice were consumed, we packed Hayden safely in the car, and they took off. The cats would return once it was quiet, grab a bite to eat, and head upstairs with me to spend the rest of the afternoon with Mama. By that time she would be worn out. Riding that lift chair was pretty tiring for an old lady. I would give her the afternoon meds, then start dinner while she enjoyed the sunset in her lift chair with both cats completely sacked out, Toes on her bed and Incha on her lap.

Sometimes Susan stopped in for kitty cocktail hour in her flannel PJ bottoms, cozy sweatshirt, and UGGS. The five of us always enjoyed the sunset and had a peaceful evening as we watched the birds take their last bath, their last drink, and their last meal before they retired to their nests for the night. A lone hummingbird arrived every evening at the same time, and we would watch his silhouette against the orange, pink and lavender sky. He drank so much sugar water, you could see his little belly extending and bubbles gurgling up in the feeder. He sat on the same perch every time and it never failed: the moment he landed, his partner arrived, nagged him, and they flew off together, only to have the same thing happen ten seconds later. It reminded me of the sitcom, *Cheers,* where Norm always sat on the same bar stool and avoided Vera's phone calls and pleas to come home. For obvious reasons, I called this hummingbird "Norm." It was a small world, but a sweet one.

Susan always stuck around and helped me get Mama ready for bed; then she moseyed on home down the hill. I stayed upstairs a little longer because I had to give Mama bedtime meds again at 10:00 p.m. before hitting the sack myself. Sundays were days that I will always treasure because it was when we had our profound mother-daughter talks, sometimes about my awesome childhood that Mama provided, and sometimes about her own traumatic childhood that her mother provided.

Mama was adopted when she was five years old. Her mother and father had divorced, and her mother remarried a man who insisted on having his own child. He forced his wife to give Mama up. For eighty-four years Mama held on to the pain of being rejected by her own mother at five years old—and who could blame her?

"What about your dad, Mama? Do you remember much

about him?" I could tell by the light in her eyes that she adored him.

"Oh yes, I idolized him. He was tall, very handsome, an impeccable dresser, and sometimes I spotted him leaning against his fancy car watching me in the schoolyard. But because the divorce and adoption were so hushed up, especially in the Catholic Church, the nuns wouldn't let me have anything to do with him. They took me to the basement of the school and hid me until he left. Nobody ever mentioned him but I knew he loved me." I grew up hearing this story, but I learned more every time I asked questions, and I think Mama liked to recollect memories of her father.

"Why couldn't you live with him, then?"

"He had no room in his life for a child. He traveled often and I think he fancied the ladies. I was in awe of him. Sometimes he brought me presents, and I still have a gold necklace and bracelet from him." I went to the closet where I had stashed a box of Mama's treasures and found the old royal blue kidney-shaped box. Nestled perfectly in a bed of white satin was a golden beaded choker. A matching bracelet was lying beside it. I picked it up, and it was obvious by its weight that it wasn't real gold. I am not sure what it was, but it was the only piece of her dad that Mama owned. I knelt down in front of her and rested my head in her lap. She stroked my hair and said, "I think he went back to Austria, where he came from, but nobody would ever talk about him. I must have a half-sibling somewhere in the world."

"I'm sorry you are so scarred by your mother's actions, Mama. But thank God you were adopted into a loving family that gave you a safe environment and an older stepsister who worshiped you." I could sense Mama's tears.

"I know dear. I am grateful for Mama and Papa and Aunt Connie. They did love me, and Aunt Connie made life fun."

I raised my head and wiped away her tears. "And now you have three children who would walk through fire for you."

"I know darling, I am fortunate."

I stood up, held her for a moment, and then gave her a kiss. I didn't want our conversation to end on a sad note, so I lightened the mood before heading to bed. "Actually, I think I would rather walk through fire than get up 4:00 a.m."

We laughed. I transferred her to her inviting bed and kissed her good night. "Sleep with the angels, Mama. I love you."

"I love you, too, darling."

I thought about her adoption and how unimaginable that pain must have been. It wasn't as if she had been an infant. At five years old, how do you not blame yourself?

I fell into bed shortly after 10:00 p.m. with my clothes still on. I desperately needed to sleep in, but if the caregiver was late and I was still asleep, Mama would miss her meds and her pain would be horrific. That was why it was so important for the caregivers to be punctual. Eventually, caregivers would be my downfall.

CHAPTER 11

One night around midnight I heard a commotion upstairs. I had been aware of it earlier, but I thought it was coming from the landlord's house next door. This time it was pretty loud, so I went upstairs and looked around. Mama was awake, so I asked her if she had heard anything. She said that she had, but it hadn't scared her. I didn't see anything, so I turned off the light, kissed her good night, and went back to bed.

Within ten minutes, Incha came through my bedroom door meowing proudly like he had caught something for me. I understood that meow so well and knew something dead or dying was in the house. I turned on the light and looked towards Incha where he sat still and looked at me, proud of his hard-earned trophy. Something moved on the floor between his paws. I flew out of bed and saw a terrified little mouse, frozen stiff with fear. I put Incha in the other room and slowly crept up on the mouse. I HAD to catch him, because there is nothing worse than a live mouse in the house, and I won't even kill a fly. I swiftly but gently cupped my hands over the mouse, expecting him to leap and fight and perhaps bite, but since he was catatonic at that point, it was easy for me to catch him. So, there I was, walking around the house in the middle of the night with a wounded mouse in my hand. I looked for a shoebox to keep him in until morning, hoping he would revive with a good night's sleep. I didn't put him outside because Toes was probably out there waiting for him.

Then I heard a very loud something scamper across the floor upstairs. There was something up there having a party for certain. I clutched the little mouse and ventured upstairs determined to find out what the heck was going on. I flipped on the switch and saw Toes, eyes as wide as saucers and black as night with ears perked as high as they could be. Both front legs were stretched to the max under a gold rag rug. At the end of his arms and paws was another lump a little larger than the one I was holding in my hand.

"Aw-w-w-w, man," was all I could think of. I explained what was going on to Mama and she laughed with delight at this midnight antic. There was no way that I could catch Toe's mouse with this one in my hand already, so I opened my jewelry box, and with one hand dumped it upside down. I watched my necklaces, bracelets, rings, and earrings crash down on the wood floor while I kept an eye on Toes and his catch-of-the-day. I set Incha's mouse in the box and closed the top. He was somewhat paralyzed, so he posed no problem. Toes meowed and looked at me proudly, still trying to reach even farther under the rug. The farther Toes reached, the farther the lump went. Then I saw a mouse's tail sticking out about two inches, so I thought, "Piece of cake, I'll just grab his tail and rescue him, too." Again, I really did not want a live mouse in the house, so I had to catch this second one. I focused on that tail and quickly grabbed it before Toes even knew what I was doing. I thought I would take him over to see Mama since his little face was so cute, but as I reached her bed (which took about three seconds), something shocking happened that I did not know about mice. Apparently, they have a defense mechanism like a lizard's, and in a split second, that mouse whirled himself around like a propeller. He spun so fast, he was just a blur, and then suddenly, his tail detached and he fell at the foot of Mama's bed between the mattress and the end board. Luckily, he was stuck. I thought Mama would die laughing at the sight of me holding just a tail and saying, "eeeeeeeuuuuuu yuk!" But I was glad he was wedged, so I grabbed him. Again, I found myself wandering around the house with a mouse in my hand, looking for more appropriate lodging. Fortunately, I glanced over to check on the other mouse and as I did, the lid was just opening and I managed to grab the escaping mouse with my free hand. Now I wandered around the house with a mouse in each hand, unable to find a box, basket, or anything to use for the night. I must have looked for a half hour. Mama took such delight in this scenario. Then I spotted a rectangular basket with a lid on it where

I kept greeting cards. With my elbows, I was able to shove all the stuff off the top of it that had accumulated over the weeks. I turned it upside down and emptied it out. Cards flew everywhere, but I did it! Next I grabbed a towel from the downstairs bathroom to line the bottom of the basket and get those little guys bedded down for the night. I spread the towel on the bottom of the basket with my elbows, and then happily and gently placed the mice in and put the lid on. Both of them were in pretty bad shape. Toes' prey had a chunk of fur taken out of his side, exposing bloody skin.

I thoroughly washed my hands, and got out the peanut butter, birdseed, and chunks of cheese. I put this feast in a jar lid and did the same with some water. Their hot tub would have to wait till morning. The truth is, I really didn't expect them to make it through the night. I put a book on top of the lid, shut them in the bathroom, and crawled into bed for the final time that night—or at least until 4:00 a.m. I slept well.

When I awoke in the morning, I went into the bathroom and cautiously lifted the lid, thinking about where I was going to bury them, or if I was just going to throw them over the fence. The first thing I saw were two little faces right up on the edge of the basket. The three of us scared each other, but I was happy that they were in good shape after all. I instantly dropped the lid and took them across the street and up the hill and let them go.

They didn't hesitate to jump out of that basket when I opened it, but the funniest thing was that both sets of cheeks were packed with the seeds, peanut butter and cheese. So the two of them scampered off looking like they had the mumps. But both stopped, turned around and took one last look at me, as if to say thanks. Either that or they were talking about me like I was nuts—the way most people do when I tell them this story.

CHAPTER 12

From the bottom of my heart, I can honestly say that nothing in my life has ever driven me to the point of insanity as much as the caregivers did. They were in my home ten hours a day, six days a week.

I painted my *Chickenware* on the dining room table next to the kitchen where the caregivers spent their time when Mama was asleep. The Chickenware had started out on a whim some years earlier when I was wandering through a Goodwill shop one afternoon. A set of four vintage juice glasses took me back to growing up in the 50s. A voice from above spoke to me and said, "Paint chickens on them." I'd never had chickens and objected, but the voice was pretty insistent and said, "Trust me." So I did. Then the glasses began to sell and before I knew it, shops coast to coast were putting in orders for *Chickenware*. I loved the time I spent painting and reflecting on Mama and the perfect "Leave It To Beaver" childhood she had created for her three beloved daughters. Sometimes my mind wandered to special efforts that Mama had made for me.

On September 6, 1964, she and Dad drove my sisters Susan and Janet, and four of my friends and me, to Detroit to a Beatles concert. At our request, they drove us by the hotel where the Beatles stayed so we could pick some grass from the lawn to tape into my Beatles scrapbook. I still have it. When the concert was over they took a carload of sweaty, crying, trembling teenagers to lunch. Mama told us that after they had dropped us off at the concert, their car passed very close to the Beatle's limousine. Mama saw Paul's face smiling out the window and he waved at her. Two years later when we saw the Beatles again, she purchased a ticket for herself.

Mama had always made Christmases perfect for us. She decorated the house so beautifully with evergreen garlands trimmed with red bows, red berries, red cardinals, red candles and tiny lights. I still feel the magic of the three of us girls coming down the stairs in red flannel pajamas and spotting Betsy Wetsy dolls in front of the fireplace next to new bicycles. Stockings were stuffed full with ribbon candy, peppermint candy canes, little stuffed animals and other goodies.

I would be lost in my reverie, when suddenly the crashing of a dish onto the tile floor, or the rattling of pots and pans would shatter my daydreams and bring me back to the real world. Water would be left running, and garbage left piling up and smelling bad because caregivers would forget to use the garbage disposal. There were days when it was impossible for me to paint. The caregivers meant well and honestly didn't do anything wrong. I should have just rented a studio or found somewhere else to paint. Frequently, to keep from lashing out, I grabbed my iPod and headed up the hill.

One afternoon after I overhead a caregiver, Debbie, talking to Mama, I couldn't stop myself from chastising her. All she talked about was herself and her life and her kids. It was nice that she interacted with Mama, but Mama really didn't respond to her because she wasn't that interested, and it was a strain for her to hear. I didn't pounce on Debbie immediately, but later when she came downstairs I had to say something. I tried to be gentle as I told her that I would prefer that she ask Mama questions about herself; that I paid her to pay attention to Mama. I wanted her to remember that there was a time when Mama was young and beautiful and talented and funny, and had roller-skated and painted incredible paintings. She was educated and had a full life as a wife, mother, daughter, sister, and artist.

"So, while you're here, please don't see her as a sick old lady," I said. "I want you to talk about her life." I showed her Mom and Dad's wedding movie from 1940 that Susan had transferred from 8mm to a DVD. It helped when the caregivers actually saw Mama young and healthy and not as a cripple with a horrible disease. I felt it was also a good exercise for Mama's brain to recall certain people, places and events. I am no doctor, but it just made sense.

The caregivers themselves thrived on doing laundry. I am very conscious of energy and utility costs, so I explained this to them and suggested they do laundry only when it was piled up. It didn't matter how often I told them though. Doing laundry appeared to be their passion.

Then there was the day the toilet flushed and water came gushing out from the base. Two hundred dollars later, it turned out that one the caregivers had put the wipes down the toilet instead of in the trash.

I will admit that it was wonderful having laundry clean and folded, and closets and drawers organized. I loved having the house sparkling clean, the decks swept every day, and the flowers deadheaded. There were definite bonuses for me as well.

I finally figured out that I could never get a grasp on what needed explaining so I explained everything—sometimes as the risk of insulting the caregivers.

While I was out one day, Susan came by and found Rowena, a caregiver, holding a hot dog on a fork over the toaster. It shocked both of us. Rowena had a husband and two little kids, and I wondered how they survived. Maybe they didn't.

Only one caregiver had a clue about cooking and that was Glenda. She could open the refrigerator and find nothing in there, but manage to put together an amazing meal for Mama—and she always made plenty for me too. Glenda usually made something Asian or Filipino, and it was consistently wonderful. But she was the only one who knew her way around a kitchen.

Of all the caregivers we had, Tara was the laziest. While the others were constantly busy, she sat around and read. No extras from Tara—and she did laundry EVERY day. It was mind-boggling to me that in the morning I would tell her that there was no need to do laundry, but by the afternoon I would hear that spin cycle. She felt entitled to help herself to my leftovers from the night before or a piece of pie that I had saved. Truth was, I didn't really mind at all, but would have preferred that she asked first. She didn't have a cell phone, so people called for her on my house phone. Sometimes I felt like her receptionist. She smoked, which was okay; but she left her butts scattered around the deck.

One afternoon I went upstairs and found Mama on the verge of tears, but it wasn't from sadness. It was from anger. Her lips were pursed and she glared at Tara, who was heading downstairs to clean up lunch dishes. When Tara was out of view Mama wrinkled her nose and stuck her tongue out at her.

"Mama, what's wrong? Didn't you like your lunch?" She had just finished a Cloud so it was hard for me to take her seriously when she had chocolate all over her mouth and hands. I grabbed a Kleenex, pulled up the wheelchair, and began to clean her up. "I don't like Tara," she muttered.

I sort of agreed. "I'm not crazy about her either, but she's only one day a week. Why? What did she do?"

Mama looked directly into my eyes. "She handed me a Cloud."

Okay, clearly I was missing something. "What do you mean? Were her hands dirty?"

"I like to pick them out of the box myself."

I could hardly take this seriously. "You're joking, right? Let me get this straight. She didn't hurt you, the lunch was good, you are clean and medicated, but you are pissed at Tara because she wouldn't let you pick your own Cloud?"

Mama took her Clouds very seriously. She would offer them to people who stopped by, but secretly hoped they would refuse. Mama was the most generous person on earth. She would give a stranger a place to bathe and sleep and offer to feed them, but when it came to Clouds, that was a different story.

"Mama, she probably figures it is easier for her to do it for you because, well, look at your fingers. They are crippled and in pain most of the time. Did you tell her that you prefer to pick your own?"

"Well, no." This was a silly conversation.

"Do you want me to tell her for you?" Mama nodded yes.

"Would you like me to bring the box over and would you like to pick out another one?" She nodded yes. I opened the clear plastic square lid and held the box close to her. With the enthusiasm of a five-year-old she reached in, and as pained as her hands were, she managed to pick the biggest Cloud and shove it directly into her mouth.

"Mama, these ladies are not mind readers. You have to use your voice and tell them what you want. They want to make you happy, but you have to tell them your needs. Okay?"

She nodded yes but she wasn't listening because her mouth was so full of chocolate, caramel, and pecans that she didn't care anymore. I kissed her forehead, went downstairs, and tactfully made the important announcement to Tara.

Tara was a whistler. She whistled along to most of the songs that came on the radio. She whistled very loudly and very off-key. It was so horrible and disturbing that it made me laugh. So, I would grab my iPod and go for a walk up the road.

Tara called one day before she left her house to announce that she was going to be a little late because she wanted to stop by the produce market and get us some fresh fruit. I told her that the point of her being there at 9:00 a.m. sharp was that I needed to sleep in because I got up at 4:00 a.m., and sometimes I didn't get back to sleep because I worried whether or not the caregiver would show up on time. "If you aren't here by nine, then consider yourself fired." Punctuality was the most important part of the job besides, of course, taking good care of Mama.

I walked a lot during those six months. I went from a size 8 pant to a size 2. You want to lose weight? Hire caregivers.

Schedules were the culprit for the most severe of my meltdowns. Just when I thought they were set, somebody needed time off or somebody's child was ill or off to college. I understood their dilemmas and tried to find replacements, but sometimes it was impossible and I had to step in too often to fill the void.

The pressure and strain quickly and constantly zapped my energy. I couldn't enjoy Mama as much anymore because I became more of a case manager and less of a daughter. The more anxiety-ridden I became, the more Mama felt like an imposition, and of course, that was the last thing I wanted. I loved Mama being there, living with me; I just didn't love all the essentials that she required. I wanted this time for her to be peaceful and joyous. Then something came along that changed my attitude.

CHAPTER 13

I was in my element: entertaining. It was Susan's birthday so I was having a party for her at my house, and was having a ball preparing food and placing bright yellow sunflowers, brilliant blue iris, and fragrant freesias around. I lit fun candles of all shapes, sizes, colors, and scents.

The pork tenderloin smelled of rosemary and raspberry pepper jelly that Susan's husband had made from berries and peppers from their garden. The house was permeated with delicious aromas. I picked my favorite homemade compilation CDs and organized them in my stereo system. I poured myself a cocktail while I set up the bar: Mandarin orange, vodka, and club soda. I felt happy and content.

I dressed Mama in a matching bright turquoise skirt and top that complimented her baby blue eyes. I wrapped her favorite silver belt around her waist, fluffed her hair, did her makeup, and clasped her pet silver circle necklace around her neck. She was quite the dish.

Mama was unable to sign anything because of her arthritic hands, so we heavily applied her hot pink lipstick so she could kiss birthday cards. This became her new signature and although a treasure to us girls, it was dispiriting to watch her penmanship revert from Catholic school perfect to shaky to illegible to lipstick kisses.

My friends Plasha, Randy, and son Hayden arrived, and they brought a young guy I'd never met. His name was Joe and he was around thirty-two years old. He didn't say much and sort of blended into the furniture, but was nice and had a fascinating career as an archeologist. The only time I remember having any interaction with him was when he came into the kitchen to refresh his cocktail, which was quite often.

It was a delightful evening. Guests grabbed their drinks and went upstairs to visit with Mama. She was charming and everyone doted over her, although she didn't enjoy long visits because it was such an effort for her to hear. When the party went back downstairs, I put "Celtic Woman" in her DVD player and left her enchanted by those gorgeous, talented women from Ireland.

After dinner I excused myself and went upstairs to prepare Mama for bed. I put her in her nightgown, patted Ponds Moisturizer all over her face, applied ChapStick on her lips, tucked her in, and kissed her good night. She was peaceful but very weary and happy to "get horizontal," as she liked to refer to it.

The party was a success and Susan had a great time.

Hayden and I danced and sang and played until he became sleepy. I put him on the guest bed, stuck in a DVD, and during the coming attractions he fell asleep.

Everybody pitched in, and within minutes the kitchen was spotless, toys put away, and coffee brewing. When Plasha, Randy and Hayden left, they asked if they could stop by the next day. They were headed to Joe's house further out in the country for the night but wanted to see us on their way home. Sounded great since the next day was "Mimosa Sunday."

I was so tired I could hardly function. I went up to check on Mama and she was sleeping soundly. I needed to get some sleep before the 4:00 a.m. alarm went off, so I had a couple hours.

I was unable to get back to sleep after that, so my behind dragged the next day when Plasha, Randy and Hayden showed up. To my surprise, their friend Joe was with them. I couldn't figure out why he came all the way back to my house since he had no plans to go in their direction, but what the hell.

Everybody was a little hungover, but I heard a cork pop and before I knew it, a mimosa was handed to me. The old "hair of the dog." It tasted pretty good. I put quiche and some fruit on the table and while they ate, I took Mama's tray up.

Hayden joined us upstairs, and that was the day that he discovered the control to Mama's hospital bed. Unlike the lift chair, Mama had to be out of the bed for this ride. Hayden had a field day. He climbed in her hospital bed and we watched him take great joy lifting the head of the bed up and down then the legs up and down. At one point he had the head all the way up and the legs all the way up and he looked like a taco. We could hardly find Hayden. I was worried Mama might die of laughter, so I kept checking her pulse to make sure she could still breathe.

Shortly after brunch everybody left, but Joe lingered for a while. This time he was animated and enthusiastic and talked about his travels and his work and inquired about my life. But I was more concerned with Mama and wasn't paying much attention to what he was saying. I really just wanted to rest.

Finally, Joe left and all I wanted to do was to fall into bed and sleep for hours but Mama was due for her 5:00 p.m. meds. I put her back into her bed and we talked about the day. Even the cats were exhausted from avoiding Hayden all afternoon. Next thing I knew, I woke up in her lift chair and her 10:00 p.m. meds were over an hour late.

Mama had been with me about four months at that point, and I was feeling the effects of sleep deprivation. The caregivers depressed me, and getting up at 4:00 a.m. became harder for me. I often put myself in Mama's place, and I felt her pain and frustration. Problem was, I felt mine too—only mine was coupled with exhaustion. This could go on another ten years. *Oh My God, how would I ever survive?*

About a week later the phone rang. "Hello?"

"Hey Beth, this is Joe, Plasha's friend. Do you remember me?"

"Sure, I remember you. You're the archeologist, right?

How could I forget? You stayed until 1:00 a.m. the other night—and came back for breakfast the next day."

"I know we stayed late and I'm sorry, but we were having such a good time."

"Yeah, it was a fun party. So what's up?"

"I was wondering if I left my hat there."

"I haven't seen it. Maybe it fell behind the couch or something. I'll ask the caregiver if she's… ya know, I clearly remember you had it on when you left. Guess it must be somewhere else."

There was silence, and then he said, "So, do you want to hang out sometime?"

My first reaction was *Is he for real?*

"Sure, you can come over and hang any time."

"Well, what are you doing now?" I had just walked in the door.

"I just got home from work and am pouring a cocktail. Why?"

"Well I'm in the area and thought I'd stop by."

I wasn't into that at the moment. I just wanted to go up and see Mama, discuss some things with the caregiver, and relax; but he had caught me off guard.

"Sure come on by for a little while. Where are you?" Hopefully with the "little while" he got the hint and wouldn't stay long.

"I am really close."

I kind of rolled my eyes.

"I just walked in the door, so give me a minute or two…"

"Okay see you soon. Bye."

I made my cocktail and headed up to see Mama. She was sitting in her lift chair looking beautiful and peaceful. Glenda was sitting next to her. I bent over and kissed Mama and greeted Glenda. I had just gotten comfortable when the doorbell rang.

"Is that Joe already?" I answered the door and it was Joe. I let him in. "That didn't take very long."

"I called from your driveway. Hope it's not too soon."

I was bewildered. "Go ahead and fix yourself a drink while I go back upstairs for a minute before the caregiver leaves. Make yourself comfortable."

I went upstairs and quietly tried to explain this guy to Mama and Glenda. They laughed as I whispered, "I have no idea what the hell this guy's doing here but I'll get rid of him." Glenda gathered her stuff and I walked with her down the stairs. "Thank you Glenda. See you tomorrow."

"Good-bye Beth."

I sat on the couch and saw that Joe had twisted up a joint. He passed it to me.

"Wanna smoke?" I thought about what responsibilities I had for the rest of the day. Mama had dinner and all her meds so she was good until 10:00 p.m. and was content watching a DVD.

"Sure. Light that puppy up."

Then he seemed a little concerned. "Will the smoke rise up and bother your mom? Does she care if you smoke?"

"Nahhhhhhh. Sometimes I blow it in her direction hoping it will help her pain. She doesn't care."

I sat on the sofa and he sat in the chair. He lit it up and

when he passed it to me, he moved over to sit next to me on the sofa. I remember thinking, *hell, it's not that far to pass the joint, but whatever.*

Joe and I talked about so many things. He was a good conversationalist and I enjoyed his company. Then suddenly he got very nervous, stood up, walked around, and said, "I have something to tell you, but it is so awkward for me."

How bad can it be? We aren't a couple, so he can't dump me. He sat back down.

"I have a huge crush on you."

"You really didn't lose your hat, did you?"

He stood up again and put his hand over his heart. "No, that was just an excuse to call you. Ever since the party I can't stop thinking about you. Your stories, your sense of humor…"

I felt like Cher in *Moonstruck.* I wanted to slap his face and yell, "Snap out of it!" I was dumbfounded and truly surprised. I did not see that coming at all. He was thirty-two and I was fifty-six.

"WHAT?" was all I could say. "What kind of crush? Like you want to take me on a date kind of crush? What's in this weed?"

"I mean it, Beth. Please let me take you on a date." He was pathetic.

"Look Joe, I'm flattered but…"

"So," he continued, "when can I take you on a date?"

"NEVER." Then I went on, "The idea is absurd. It's not gonna happen."

"Look Beth, I admit that I am not good in relationships

but…"

"RELATIONSHIPS? Have you been drinking bong water? There is NOT, nor will there ever be, a relationship developing here. Even if it did make sense, I have no room in my life for a kid right now. My commitment is to Mama. My plate is full. My energy is zapped, I don't sleep, my appetite is gone, I constantly worry and second-guess, and I don't see any relief in sight for a loooooong time. Now where would I put you?"

At that moment we heard a thunderous snore from Mama and then I looked up at Joe.

"Did I mention I don't sleep?"

Joe was not going to take no for an answer. "So when do you want to go on our date?"

It was as if he hadn't heard a word I said.

"There is a twenty-four year age difference between us. I bet you haven't even seen *Gone With The Wind,* have you?"

He looked quite puzzled. "No."

"Well, there ya go. You're too young."

"What? Just because I haven't seen a stupid movie you won't go out with me?"

I was getting weary of this.

"No I won't go out with you because…"

"Because what?"

"Because I don't have the energy and you're too young. End of discussion."

He was persistent. "Look Beth, I feel a real connection with you. Even though there is an age difference, we have a lot in common."

"Like what? What do we have in common?" I was getting agitated now and feeling like it was time to put Mama in her bed. Luckily, Glenda had already put her in her nightclothes.

"Like both of us have traveled and lived all over the world. We love adventures and exotic places. You have a great sense of humor. What you're doing for your mom is a tremendous undertaking and I have a lot of respect for you. Please just let me take you to dinner. You deserve to be taken out and pampered for an evening. We'll sit in front of a fireplace and order a nice bottle of wine..."

"Champagne—the most expensive!"

"Wednesday?" Joe had a twinkle in his eye. "We'll also rent a movie."

I surrendered. "Pick me up at 6:00. You pick the restaurant; I'll pick the movie."

Joe jumped on the couch with joy. "Really? You'll go out with me?"

I pulled him down to my level. "Don't get too excited, kid. I love fine champagne. Don't expect any making out, hand jobs, blow jobs, or sex. Now go home. Mama needs tending to and I am worn out."

Joe headed for the door, turned around, kissed me on the cheek and said, "I promise you'll have a night to remember."

I pushed him out the door. "LEAVE!"

As I climbed the stairs I made a mental note to myself: Call the video store and reserve *Gone With The Wind*.

The kid picked me up in his mother's Mercedes sports car convertible and showed up with the most pitiful, scraggy little branch of red roses that I had ever seen. He probably picked it from a bush in his yard or his neighbor's. I was touched by the gesture, though, and appreciated the "Charlie Brown" flowers.

Joe took me to a high-end restaurant about four miles away, and we sat outside and watched the moon rise and the stars pop out. He and I were never at a loss for words. We talked about a million different things and we obviously enjoyed each other's company. Both of us had traveled to exotic and remote places all over the world and had an appreciation for other cultures and tropical waters. I had lived in Indonesia when I was his age and couldn't get enough adventure in my life. I still can't. His work took him to those wonderful places too—but he got paid for it.

When the temperature dropped, we moved over to the warm fireplace that was built from river rocks and enjoyed the last of our bottle of champagne and conversation by the heat and glow. It was a wonderful, romantic evening, and I forgot about the age difference. I embraced every second and lived in the moment. Most of the time my mind was constantly consumed with Mama, so this was a great distraction, even if it was just for the night.

Suddenly, I sprang up and asked Joe what time it was. When he answered "ten," I panicked and told him that I had to get home for the 10:00 p.m. meds. We were out of there in five minutes.

Upon our arrival I heard rock and roll blasting from my house and every light was on. I flew upstairs only to find Susan and Mama rocking out to an old Roy Orbison concert that was on PBS. It had been recorded years ago with Bruce Springsteen, Tom Waits, Elvis Costello, Jackson Brown, k. d. lang, Bonnie Raitt, and others. It was a fabulous concert and one of Mama's favorites. Even the cats were enjoying it; Toes on Susan's lap, and Incha snuggled next to Mama. Susan hung out for a little while, and then headed home. She had given Mama her meds, and I realized then that I was beginning to come apart— we had talked about her taking care of the meds and putting Mama to bed, and it had completely slipped my mind. I kissed Mama good night and tucked her in.

"Sleep with the angels, Mama, I love you."

"I love you, too, darling. Good night."

Joe and I went downstairs for a nightcap and more conversation. I was in the kitchen making our drinks when he grabbed me, hugged me, told me that he had a great time and planted an unexpected kiss on my lips that shot all thoughts of diapers and meds out the window. It was long, passionate, wonderful, and sent me right to my happy place. We sat on the couch and proceeded to make out like teenagers. It felt wonderful being in a man's arms again, feeling biceps through his shirt and having a sense of being rescued from what was beginning to feel a bit traumatic with Mama.

It was getting late, and as wonderful as the evening had been, I was not about to have sex with this kid. I informed him of that and kicked him out. That 4:00 a.m. alarm was not going to go away; and the late night with Joe, as much as I had enjoyed it, was adding to my sleep deprivation. I collapsed into bed and purred like a kitten as I reflected on the evening, even though I could feel myself spiraling downward.

Joe called the next day and told me he had a great time and asked when we could get together again. For the next couple of weeks he stopped by often and, to be honest, he boosted my energy. It was kind of nice to have somebody pay that kind of attention to me. I felt raw and vulnerable from fatigue, caregivers, balancing finances, and making major decisions. It depleted my energy mentally as well as physically and spiritually. All of it was beginning to accumulate, so Joe's interest and company was welcome even if it was crazy.

One Saturday there was a huge party in his community. He told me that Plasha and Randy and Hayden were going with him and would then spend the night at his house. He wanted me to come but he knew I had the Mama thing. He said maybe he would stop by on following day on "Mimosa Sunday" because Plasha and Randy were certain to.

"Cool. See you Sunday," was how I left it and felt a little sad that I couldn't join my friends for the party.

Early Sunday I awoke to a bloodcurdling wail around 2:00 a.m. I went running up to Mama, skipping two steps at a time, and found Incha asleep on her sore leg. I removed him, but her pain was agonizing. I doubled the painkiller and gave it to her before 4:00 a.m. Then I sat with her, rubbed her forehead, and waited for the pills to take effect. Nothing helped and she went from moaning to crying, then sobbing so loud that she shook. I crawled into bed and held her in my arms. Her eyes were swollen from the crying and her shoulders felt bony as I wrapped myself around her.

"Please darling, if you love me put the pillow over my face." Her sobs were so severe I could hardly understand her through her hiccupped breathing. "I can't go on like this. I am begging you, please just end it for me." Her frail little hands were clutching my robe. It would have been so easy for me to just gently place the pillow over her face and ease all this suffering, but as much as I agonized for her, I couldn't do it. I held her tighter and tried to calm her but no words could console the pain, so I gently stroked her head as tears streamed down my cheeks.

By now Incha was back, overly concerned and wanting to be with her. He really took this caregiving thing very seriously. It wasn't fair that Mama had to endure so much. She had been so brave and good-natured during all of it.

Finally, Mama dozed off and slept peacefully. I fell back into bed around 5:00, well aware that it was Sunday and I would be with her all day with no caregiver. This was the first Sunday that I was not up for "Mimosa Sunday." I was completely depleted and wished I could think of a way to end Mama's suffering. I couldn't get the vision and sound of her pleas out of my thoughts. How much longer can she go on like this? How much does she have to suffer? What is the right thing to do?

I kind of hoped that something would happen and no one would come by on Sunday. I really just wanted to stick close to Mama in case she needed extra pills if the agonizing pain resurfaced.

As it turned out, it was a short "Mimosa Sunday," which

suited me just fine. Plasha, Randy and Hayden were soon off to an event. Joe had showed up too and intended to join them. He said that he wished that I could go but when I explained to him what kind of a night I had with Mama he insisted on keeping me company. I went upstairs to check on Mama and she was still sleeping peacefully. Honestly I wanted to crawl into the lift chair next to her and sleep, but I was suddenly feeling energy—sexual energy—from the kid and it revived me.

Mama slept most of the day. I woke her for her meds and snacks but she was so spent from the night before that I just let her fall back to sleep.

I went downstairs and we smoked some weed and had a cocktail, which took the edge off. As much as I wanted him to stay, I wanted him to leave. He stayed. The truth is, I wanted to make love, but I would rather it be under better circumstances because I didn't feel connected to my body anymore. Mentally, I knew that if we had sex, a part of me wouldn't be present and it would be a big mistake.

CHAPTER 14

So the kid and I had sex. I had resisted for months, but I had no fight left in me.

After dinner we ended up on the floor making out. I was lost in the moment with no thoughts of Mama, caregivers, or medications, when I felt Joe's long muscular arms reach behind my back. He forcibly scooped me up and carried me to the bedroom and laid me on the bed. I knew how Scarlet O'Hara felt when Rhett grabbed her and carried her up that staircase and the next day she couldn't stop smiling and singing. (Joe never did see the movie.)

He gently sat me up, unbuttoned my shirt and nuzzled his face in my small but responsive breasts. Then slowly he reached down to my jeans and began to unzip them when...Oh my God!! I remembered that just below my hipbone was an estrogen patch that screamed *I'm old and menopausal! My eggs are dried up and every hair on my head is dyed!* I completely freaked out. No way was I going to let him see this patch. So I pushed him down on the bed, climbed on top, straddled him and slowly lifted his t-shirt over his head until it covered his eyes. Then I held it there as I reached down my pants and ripped off the patch. But when I ripped it off, it stuck to my fingers like dental floss. I shook my hand several times but it wouldn't fall off. Finally, I rubbed it along the sheets and it unstuck just as Joe's eyes were revealed. He pulled me on top of him, and as I sat on his stomach I looked up towards heaven in ecstasy; then I looked down at Joe and abruptly remembered to not look down with my head, only my eyes, or gravity would pull my entire fifty-six-year old loose face down to his chest like a 100-pound weight. I looked back up and thought, "God, I wish I had booked that face-lift."

I was frustrated that I couldn't get out of my head. So far the sex was pretty lame, and it was my fault. I wanted to make this a special night, especially since I made Joe wait so long. I decided to wiggle my body down his long legs and go for what men love most. I remembered the 70s book, *The Sensuous Woman* by "J." She taught us all those "maneuvers" like the "Hoover" that were guaranteed to make men buy you diamond earrings if you stopped midway. I slowly kissed and nibbled my way down his chest and belly, trying to decide on the "Silken Swirl" or the "Butterfly Flick." But when I arrived at my destination I realized my mouth and throat were so dry from the champagne and pot that— well, to quote Marilyn Monroe, "I was spitting cotton." I couldn't have sucked a Popsicle, I was so dehydrated. I asked Joe to pass me the water bottle on the nightstand, and when he rolled over, there was the estrogen patch stuck to his butt! Oh My God! There was no way I could perform any maneuver now because I almost died holding back laughter. I wondered if he'd grow breasts.

In the meantime, Joe decided he'd be the young buck and aggressively take the bull by the horns. He rolled me over on my back and slowly worked his way down my tiny body, kissing and stroking every nook and cranny in his path. I was finally and completely lost in our sensuality.

Suddenly, as if a bomb had gone off upstairs, Mama let out a loud half SNORT! Joe stopped. I stopped. I lifted myself up on my elbows. We looked up towards Mama's room then at each other, frozen, and waited.

"Did she die? Is this it?" We waited. Mama exhaled. We exhaled. Mama continued with soft steady breaths and things were back on track. It took me a minute, but once again I transcended into seventh heaven.

Soon, and without warning, I was distracted by a tiny tickle that started to irritate my nose. I tried to ignore it in hopes that it was my imagination. I even tried a very soft, quiet sniff, but it didn't help. In fact it became worse. A little drip from one nostril started, then a drip from the other nostril, and before I knew it I was having a damn allergy attack and Niagara Falls was running out my nose. What next? Well, next I felt a sneeze slowly build and build and build and build. Joe raised his head and watched as an "AWWCHOOO" of volcanic proportions damn near blew both of us off the bed. Joe rolled over and grabbed me a tissue. Instinctively I looked for the patch on his butt but couldn't quite tell if it was still there. I asked him to reach in the drawer and get the nasal spray. He handed me the spray and sat next to me. I waited for a clear passage in my nose, then quickly snorted the spray before it plugged up again. Joe held me in his arms and I apologized several times, embarrassed as we listened to Mama's steady snoring.

Toes, my cat, was having a blast batting around and stalking the entire box of wet, wadded up balls of tissue that were scattered all over the floor. I thought about a late night talk show I'd seen once with Ellen DeGeneres. She was very sad because she and Anne Heche had just broken up, and she showed a short film about cat toys that she had invented. They were just wadded-up tissue balls from all her crying, and her cats had started to play with them. Ellen was definitely onto something. Eventually the nasal spray kicked in and my nose dried up. Thank God!

Joe began to stroke my back and kiss my neck and I got turned on again. We lay back down on the bed and Joe climbed on top of me as he kissed my shoulders and waiting lips. I let out heavy sighs of passion through my nose, and as soon as I did that, I thought I heard something. I wasn't sure what I heard or even if it came out of me so I exhaled again. Holy Crap! Now my nose was whistling! I wasn't certain if Joe heard it, but I swear, I could have whistled the entire Beatles *White Album* through one nostril. Joe tried to be nonchalant and not let me know that it bothered him. He kissed me again, and when a high pitched shrill of a train whistle pierced both our ears, Joe doubled up in hysteria. In fact, he laughed so hard he fell off the bed and rolled from side to side on the floor laughing in the sea of wet tissue balls.

I could have said, "Yeah you laugh now, kid, but who's the one with the estrogen patch stuck to his booty? Huh?" But I didn't say anything. I just sat there whistling.

Suddenly Joe pulled me down into the sea of tissues and asked, "So can you whistle 'Rocky Raccoon'?"

"What key?"

He grabbed me and said, "There's nothing left to go wrong now." And he kissed me. All of a sudden the alarm clock blasted louder than my nose. Four a.m. Time for Mama's meds.

CHAPTER 15

The kid left just before dawn, and that morning the caregiver did not show up. I was exasperated. No phone call, nothing. Enraged, I called her cell phone and got her voicemail. She called me back a few minutes later and told me that she was in the ER with her son. It was a common cold and he was fine. She said she would be there around 11:00.

"Never mind showing up now. As a matter of fact, never mind showing up again at all. I am so sorry, but I need somebody who will be here on time every day or at least call before the shift." I could tell she was upset. I was harsh, but the truth was that it was not an emergency and she could have called. I knew that she lived with her mother and grandmother who could easily have taken her son in or called me.

So, I was the caregiver that day. I was so fatigued and distraught that I sat down and sobbed and sobbed for quite a while. The thought of training yet another caregiver was staggering. And would she be able to cook?

A frustrating aspect about caregiving for Mama was the never ending second-guessing. *Am I too harsh with the caregivers? Am I too lenient with the caregivers? What would Mama like to eat? Should we change her meds? Does that look like the beginning of a bedsore? Will this caregiver work out? Will she show up on time? Will she show up? Will the money hold out? Are we low on supplies?* Second-guessing never stops! It can drive one insane, and I had already traveled that road two months ago.

A new development in my health had occurred. Even though I was on estrogen replacements (I switched from the patch to a pill), I got dreadful night sweats. I woke up in the middle of the night drenched from the top of my head to my waist. I had to dry my hair with a hair dryer, sometimes change my sheets, and always change my nightgown. Sometimes it happened twice in one night. If I woke up drenched around 4:00 a.m., I could handle it because I had to get up anyway, but this rarely occurred at convenient times. I was a mess. The night sweats continued for another nine months.

I started smoking cigarettes and lost my appetite. I power walked up the hill almost every day so rapidly that I lost more weight too. Kitty cocktail hour started earlier and lasted longer. My mantra went from *God get me through this, God get me through this,* to *HELP!!!* I started smoking pot too, and between cigarettes and joints, I reeked.

My *Chickenware* business slacked off, and it was just as well because I hated painting in my own home now. Creativity was the last thing on my mind. I was descending deeper and deeper into my own pity party when suddenly one morning a light went on. "Get a grip, Beth, The day will come when Mama won't be here, so buck up, get over yourself, and turn that negative energy around. You won't get a chance to do it over." So I pulled myself together. I knew what I had to do. The kid had to go. I had no room or energy for him.

Later that same afternoon Mama was in her lift chair and wanted to get horizontal. I put her in the wheelchair and pushed her to the side of the bed. I did a "one, two, three" and lifted her, but as I lowered her, the bed rolled away from us and I was unable to stop the fall. What I was able to do, however, was break it. We went down together in slow motion; and in the process, I maneuvered my body around and under her so she would fall on top of me. After a relatively soft landing, I was on the bottom and she was on top and we were nose to nose. I was pretty certain that she was okay—and was completely certain when she looked into my eyes, smiled and said, "Hi." She was so funny; and more importantly, she wasn't scared. Through some miracle and lots of super strength, I gently lifted her off to the side and left her there until I could stand and pull her up by her armpits.

Sometimes Mama didn't realize she could bend her knees and had a tendency to keep them locked. "Mama, for God's sake, what are you? A giraffe? Could you bend your knees and help me out a little here?"

With that, both of us laughed and I had to set her down again until our giggling stopped. "OK, let's try this again. Now, bend your knees—one, two, three and up we go." That time we were successful. I got her into bed along with the cats, and kissed her. She looked at me and said, "I'm proud of you, darling."

I looked at her and was suddenly overwhelmed by how fortunate I felt to have such an incredible Mama. I had to tell her.

"Mama, you amaze me. For a person who had such a rough beginning in life, you are the most loving, understanding, supportive mother a child could have. I feel so blessed."

She looked a little puzzled. "What brought this on?"

I pulled up the wheelchair and sat. I found her hand under the covers and held it.

"I've decided to stop seeing the kid." I predicted how she would react. "It's not because of you. Don't worry. The bottom line is that it's a dead-end relationship anyway."

Her eyes were sad. "Darling I can move to an…"

I interrupted her instantly. "No, Mama. It would never last. Besides… truthfully? I would rather get some sleep than spend energy on a doomed relationship."

"Oh darling I feel so bad."

"Mama, don't feel bad. It's just a matter of time before he falls for some young girl his own age, which is best because he wants kids and I am clearly too old for that. Anyway, he recently mentioned a student apprentice that he has taken on. She is going on his next dig with him. I have a feeling that… well, trust me. I'll get over him but I don't know how much time I have with you. And you are where my love lies right now. You are more important to me than the kid will ever be."

"Well if you really feel that way, but . . ."

"Exhaustion is overtaking my enthusiasm for him. I can't share things with him that I could with somebody closer to my age. Besides, he didn't know who Bobby Darin was."

"Oh, then you better dump him."

"Or Louis Armstrong."

"Oh heavens! You must end this." We laughed.

"And, he hasn't even seen *Gone With The Wind.*"

"Do you feel sad about it?"

"Nahh, I just want some sleep. I want to be rested for you because I treasure this time we have together. Guys come and go, but you are my Mama. Truthfully, I'm not really enjoying the time I spend with him anymore."

"He did recognize a light in you that all of us see and adore. He is smart for that."

Mama let go of my hand and held out her arms. "Oh my darling, I love you so. Thank you for telling me that." We embraced for quite a while. I tucked Mama in and kissed her good night.

I crawled into bed, and reflected on my loving childhood a little longer, then thought about the task at hand. I knew Joe would be home tomorrow. I decided I would drive out and drop the bomb in person.

The next morning Glenda showed up on time. I prepared what I was going to say to Joe while taking my shower. I looked in the mirror, fluffed myself up and tried desperately to not look like I had been up for four months, but the truth was, I was running on empty. I looked and felt as if somebody had stuck a straw in me and sucked out all my blood and energy.

My face was thin and gaunt, the circles around my eyes were dark and deep, and my brow was constantly furrowed. The biggest shock was when I saw my spine sticking out all the way down my back. Thank God I was about to make some changes.

I rehearsed what I was going to say to Joe over and over.

My instincts told me that it wouldn't be a crushing blow to him. I knew all the Mama stuff wasn't easy, and I appreciated the attraction, but it was time to move on.

I decided to go out to his house unannounced. I needed an outing, and he had given directions and his address to me once when I thought I would get away, but never had.

I drove up his long driveway in the country for the first time, and was a little uncertain that I was in the right place. I passed his guesthouse, and as I approached the main house something remarkable and eerie happened. All the color drained out of the scene. It was as if I had wandered into the *Wizard of Oz* before Dorothy went somewhere over the rainbow. The yard was barren and brown because it was summer and very dry. There were no blossoms anywhere, no pots of flowers, and no green leaves on the trees. I entered the house through the kitchen and found the same thing: the walls were dull, the counters were bare, and there was no red, green, yellow, or bright blue anywhere. It was shocking. The living room had a dull beige carpet with a huge black stain. The furniture was drab and there was nothing happy throughout the entire house. The only sign of "life" was a huge photo of a dinosaur skeleton that hung on the wall. I looked out the dirty window, and suddenly a family of quail came running out of a bush. My sense was that they were probably looking for a happier environment to raise their young.

I didn't see any sign of the kid anywhere and the house was silent. I found my way down the hall and was just about to call him when I heard a faint whimper. It sounded like a kitten in distress. I stopped and listened. I tiptoed closer to the sound, which led past a room full of photos, fossils, skulls and excavation tools. It seemed to come from what I assumed was his bedroom. The door was open. The sound became louder as I peeked in. Joe was there—and not alone.

My instincts had told me that he may be interested in his new apprentice and now I was certain.

I leaned against the door, swallowed, then ducked back into the shadow and thought about what to do. I had come all the way up here to end it anyway so I thought about whether I should confront him or just quietly turn and leave. I wasn't quite sure how I felt. Actually, I was a little relieved that I didn't have to make my prepared speech after all. In fact I was thrilled that I didn't have to do anything but turn around and leave. An important lesson that I have learned in my lifetime is that we are capable of changing our attitude. Too many times we choose to be angry or sad or ill, and we hang on to it when all along we own the power to be forgiving, joyful, and healthy—and that was the choice I decided to make.

I was much too exhausted for drama anyway.

I felt uplifted, relieved, and happy when I drove off. I passed the quail, thought about bringing them with me, then continued on down the road. Life was back in Technicolor! I couldn't wait to tell Mama.

CHAPTER 16

Mama was sitting in her lift chair when I returned from Joe's, and I greeted her with a huge hug and kiss. She was bursting with curiosity.

"Oh darling, how did it go?"

I pulled the commode close to her lift chair, took a seat, and said, "Nothing like I thought it would. Listen to this." I told Mama the story, and then I realized that it was kitty cocktail hour. I went downstairs and made myself a cocktail and grabbed a bag of Pepperidge Farms goldfish crackers and some cheese. I threw away the remaining cigarettes and cancelled the call to replenish my pot stash.

Mama and I listened to Bobby Darin and watched Russell the crow, Norm the hummingbird, and life on the deck. I offered Mama a goldfish cracker and popped a couple in my mouth. Mama stopped mid-chew, scrunched up her face, and said, "These are really hard."

Surprised, I looked at her and said, "No, Mama, they shouldn't be. Spit it out."

I held my hand under her mouth, and a tooth landed in the center of my palm.

"Mama, you lost a tooth." I saw panic and fear in her eyes. "Let me look in your mouth." I opened the drawer next to her bed and grabbed the little flashlight and took a look. "Does it hurt?"

She shook her head no.

"Well, I don't see any blood or swelling. It was just an old tooth that made a clean break."

Tears welled up in her eyes, and terrified, she said, "A dentist won't make a house call. What are we going to do?"

I looked deep into those eyes, wiped her tears with my fingers, smiled, and said, "We're gonna put it under the pillow and see what the tooth fairy brings."

She laughed at my unexpected answer. She realized that if I thought it was serious, I would be taking action and calling the dentist. She lit up and said, "I wonder what the tooth fairy brings an eighty-nine-year-old woman."

Laughing, I answered, "Guess we'll just have to wait and see."

The next morning before the caregiver arrived I woke Mama to see what the tooth fairy brought her.

"Mama, wake up. Time for your meds." My hand reached under her pillow.

She opened her eyes and was delighted to see my face instead of a caregiver's. I pulled two Clouds out from under her pillow and held them up for her to see. "Oh my God, does the tooth fairy know you or what? Look what she brought you!"

She squealed with joy and we both laughed.

"Now you can rot out another tooth." It was a great way to start the day. If I had reacted with panic the day before, things would have been scary for her. With humor, I was able to raise her out of her fear and sorrow. It was the only way to be a caregiver.

I realized then that caregivers set the tone. If I was out of sorts, then Mama assumed she was responsible and felt like an imposition. That was the last thing I wanted. It was important to put on a happy face. I desperately needed a few nights away, but that never happened. No one ever offered to spend the night for me so I could get some rest. But that was okay; this was my decision and I really wanted to do it graciously. The past six months with Mama hadn't been about expectations or judging others. Everybody had supported me in ways that their strengths would allow. It wasn't fair to take on a task, then get upset when friends and family didn't jump in to help.

My goal was to live in an evolved, spiritual state of grace where there was no ego; where I was able to transcend exhaustion, fear, loneliness, desperation, and judgment. I wanted to rise above myself and exist in a higher state of consciousness, but I felt I was being tested by the powers that be every day, and every day I was growing weaker and weaker. My focus was only on Mama. When I became overwhelmed in negativity, I took deep breaths, repeated my mantra, found my center, and transformed my attitude to positive. I had to take care of myself so I could be there for Mama.

I looked at the clock. It was 9:45. The caregiver was either forty-five minutes late or a no-show. I called her on her cell and there was no answer. I hadn't slept much the night before and in spite of Joe being out of the picture, I was still fatigued. Now I felt defeated and weary; I was even too tired to be angry. *God get me through this, God get me through this...* I wanted to go outside and scream at the top of my lungs, but I took deep breaths, thought of how innocent Mama was, found my center, and calmed down. The caregiver called and said that she had a flat tire and that she would be there in twenty minutes. I didn't have the strength to question or confront her. I was too relieved that she was coming at all to be upset.

I needed to hike up a mountain. I'd gone downstairs to get my daypack when I heard a very weird noise outside the guest bedroom's door. It was sort of a hissing sound, but not like a cat. I slowly ventured outside and there was Toes herding a huge gopher snake. The snake was about four feet long and coiled up with his eyes fixed on Toes. Toes walked around him, and then lay down in a Cleopatra-like pose. Then he got up and wandered around the snake again. The snake's long angular head followed Toes, and then he hissed. Gopher snakes move their tails to mimic rattlesnakes, but Toes wasn't too impressed and got up to antagonize the snake again.

Gopher snakes, however, do bite. They are not venomous, but they could puncture a kitty. I picked Toes up, much to his humiliation, and put him in the house. A vet bill was the last thing I needed. I wanted to pick up the snake and bring him in to show Mama, but Glenda was deathly afraid of snakes and if he got loose in the house, she would have raced back to the Philippines in one leap. I guided him off the driveway and into the brush, and then I headed up the hill.

I didn't take my iPod this time because I wanted to reflect on my situation with Mama. She was very perceptive, and we were so tuned into each other that I knew she sensed my despair and frustration and saw how thin and gaunt I had become. I could tell Mama was beginning to feel confined upstairs. Even though it was a large, beautiful, sunny room, it must have felt smaller and smaller to her everyday. I needed to make some changes that would be best for both of us, but I wasn't sure how. I prayed and prayed and watched for signs of a miracle.

That night I dozed off listening to Mama's high-pitched kitty voice echoing throughout the house, "Incha, Incha, baby cat, where are you? Come here, kitty, kitty, kitty." That always brought tears to my eyes because it was so endearing. But, the amazing thing was that Incha heard her, and even though he was getting older and it was difficult for him to make the jump onto her bed, he always found a way to get in and settle with her every time she beckoned him. Incha, the old soul, could comfort her in a way now that I couldn't. He was a class act. He was my Master. Scenes like that made all the 4 a.m. alarms worth it, and I slept with a smile on my face.

That in itself was a miracle, but I needed a bigger one.

CHAPTER 17

Deepak Chopra says, "The more miracles you recognize, the more they come to you." I truly believed that because I lived a miracle. When I looked back on the last six months and all that had occurred; and then how I had ended up renting a place from wonderful landlords that was perfect for Mama (with the beautiful French doors and the walk-in shower large enough to accommodate a wheelchair), it could only have been Divine Intervention. I felt blessed and honored to have rescued Mama and had her safe with me.

I pulled out my tarot cards to seek guidance. I lit some aromatherapy candles, did some stretches to open up my chakras, and then spread the cards out on my worktable. I realized that I wasn't in an emotional or mental state to handle any bad news such as how my life could go on like this for another ten years or that I may never have good sex again. I closed my eyes and prayed to Quan Yin, Blessed Mother,

Buddha, Dad, and anybody I thought could help. Then I took all the negative cards out of the deck before I started. That was one way to avoid a dire reading. No point in taking unnecessary risks. Then I gathered the cards up, shuffled them, cut them and spread them.

I heard a clear message. Don't stay stuck in negativity, anger, or fear; they are toxic. Turn all negative thoughts into positive ones, or the guidance will be blocked and I will not be receptive. Keep my heart open and release angst and worry. I heard that "If you change the vibes you can change reality." It became clear to me that when I was off my center, I needed to breathe, release negative energy, open my heart, and name three things that I was grateful for. Okay. Now it was time to go meditate on it.

I changed into my hiking boots and drove about five miles to Garland Ranch, a wonderful regional park in Carmel Valley, with over 4,400 acres of wilderness along an ever-flowing river. There are ponds, springs, waterfalls, dense chaparral, and spectacular vistas that make the strenuous hikes well worth it. In the summer when water is scarce the mountain lions come down to the river, and warning signs are often posted to be aware of them. I've always loved it there.

When I arrived, the parking lot was full, but the great thing about that park is that once you start to hike, you rarely see anybody. I wanted to be alone so I would recognize that miracle I was so desperately in search of.

It was a hot, sunny, summer day. I crossed the bridge over the river and stopped to watch a pair of mallard ducks casually swimming and chatting with each other. Little baby trout and sticklebacks were hanging out just under the surface of the clear water. Then I continued my journey.

Hawks flew and screeched high above me, and the amusing trill of a mockingbird made me laugh and think of Mama. The cottonwood trees were completely leafed out, and in the rolling meadow, tall pale green and golden grasses were ruffling in the soft breeze. The sky was an intense shade of blue with snow-white puffy clouds. I felt warm and happy and content as I always do when I'm out in nature. It was a perfect day.

I hiked up to the waterfall but there was no water. We needed rain. Iridescent blue and black butterflies danced together in the sunlight, crossing each other's paths, and I was mesmerized by their shadows. A ladybug landed on my pack and hung out with me for a moment. The smell of the bay laurel trees combined with the damp, earthy aroma of emerald green soft moss filled the area. I drank some cool water from my bottle, then headed further up the mountain.

I arrived on top of the world, opened my arms, looked towards the sky, let the sun massage my face, and took long deep breaths. Then I walked a little farther to a pond that was very still, and the reflection of the sky, clouds, grasses and trees took my breath away. A great blue heron landed on the bank and we gazed at each other, engaging in a spiritual conversation. There was nobody around but us. It was calming, yet energizing. I sat on the edge of the pond and reflected on the past six months with Mama.

I embraced that moment and felt God's presence all around me: in the sky, trees, butterflies, hawks, mockingbird, ladybug, great blue heron, pond—everywhere. I felt closer to God in nature than in any man-made structure. This was my church. Every sense of my being was fulfilled. It reminded me of my favorite line from a John Denver song that goes, "You fill up my senses, like a night in the forest."

Then in my silent and peaceful state, a light flashed over my head and I was struck with a brilliant idea. Suddenly, my prayers were answered. I gathered up my hiking paraphernalia and acted on my miracle. The birds felt my energy shift and sang louder, and the heron flew off. The breeze became a wind and the aromas changed with each step. It was as if I had wings, the way I flew down the mountain. Life was changing. Even my water tasted sweeter. I drove home filled with enthusiasm and joy.

The house smelled of garlic and ginger when I got home. I plopped down my purse, pack, and water and greeted Glenda as she cooked dinner, then raced up the stairs two at a time. I couldn't wait to give Mama news that would change both of our lives. As I approached the top step, Incha, aroused by my enthusiasm, jumped off Mama's bed and reached the top of the stairs at the same time I did. I tripped over him and went flying into the middle of the room.

Mama shot me a puzzled look and held back laughter as she observed me face down, spread eagle on the hardwood floor.

"Are you ok?" she giggled.

"Yes, I'm fine," I reassured her as I gathered myself and stood up. "We need to talk."

Her curiosity was piqued but she couldn't quite get the

image of me sprawled all over the floor out of her head and laughed again. Incha, who was obviously fine, came over to make sure I was alright. I pulled the wheelchair close to Mama, took a seat, looked her straight in the eye and said, "Mama, I know that you haven't been very happy here for the last few weeks. I know that I am spending less time with you and more time stressed and frustrated with either the caregivers, the physical therapists, or dealing with food."

Mama listened. "Go on, dear." She was still holding back laughter.

"Well, I also realized that you never get a change of scenery here. We can't put you in the wheelchair and walk around the neighborhood like we did when you were in assisted living places. You're just too confined here." I could tell that she agreed with me, but she didn't want to hurt my feelings.

"Well, I know this is very hard on you, too, darling."

"Mama, I'm not going to lie to you, because, well, I can't. You know me too well. You're right, this is pretty hard on me, but it's not you, it's the stuff that comes with it. I don't feel like a daughter anymore. I feel more like your case manager. Having to stay on top of everything is taking its toll on both of us. I love you so much and the most important thing in my life is to make your life as happy and healthy as I can."

"I know, dear, and you've been amazing. I don't know how you do all that you do."

"I do it because I love you, but guess what?"

Her turquoise eyes widened.

"You are in great shape now. Your sores are completely

healed, your vitals are strong, we figured out your meds, and you look fabulous. How would you feel about going back into assisted living if we find the perfect one, perhaps with men?"

"I will do whatever you want me to, dear."

"No, Mama. I want you think about it."

"Well, I am sort of tired of the same old scenery."

"Ok, I'm going to make some calls and find the most beautiful place on the Peninsula. I promise you, I will only move you somewhere spectacular with good people, close to us. Otherwise, you will stay here and we will make it work."

"Well, it sounds good, dear, but where do you think you will find something? And will they be able to handle me?"

I got nose-to-nose with her and said, "Mama, we have been blessed with so many miracles already. Let's trust that the perfect place will manifest itself."

"Okay, darling."

I hugged her and kissed her and went for the phone.

Once the idea sunk in, Mama was excited at the prospect of a change.

I called our beloved friend, Shary. She knew every facility in the area. Shary said, "Beth, if I ever have to go into a facility, this would be the one."

That was good enough for me. Within fifteen minutes, I called the place. Turns out, there was a long waiting list, so I phoned Shary back and gave her the distressing news.

We hung up and within five minutes, she returned the call and said, "They are waiting for your call."

Shary is amazingly compassionate. When you pass on, if you find yourself south instead of north, just mention her name and you will get the express elevator to the top.

The next day, Susan, Janet, and I visited Poppy Garden Villa. It was fabulous. Nothing like the "Cuckoo's Nests" we had visited in the past. Lilly, a little Corgi-Poodle mix, greeted us when we entered. A scrumptious-smelling chicken was roasting with rosemary and garlic, and warm brownies were cooling on the bright yellow and blue kitchen counter. There were only six residents, so it was homey and comfortable.

Mama's room was at the end of the hall on the right. The walls were a pretty pale pink and the room was warm and bright. French doors graced with flowing white sheers exited to a wonderful large deck. Mama loved pink and she loved sheers. Beyond the deck was a pasture with a white horse that came to visit. The trees were loaded with birds of all kinds, but it was the quail that congregated to check us out. You couldn't see a structure or a person. It was beautiful and private. The owner, Julia, was a nurse and lived on the premises, which was a plus. The caregivers were young, experienced, helpful, and fun. We chatted with Julia for a while and explained Mama's condition to her. This was an assisted living facility, which meant that the residents must be fairly mobile. Julia assured us that the girls were used to lifting disabled patients and were very capable.

"Mama needs to be fed, dressed, lifted on and off the toilet, and have her teeth brushed. She also needs to have her meds sorted out and dispensed. She has very little use of her hands and even less of her feet." Julia said they were licensed for one immobile resident.

"I can come to your house and evaluate her tomorrow if

you like."

"Well, first I would like to bring Mama over today to see it and make sure she approves."

"Of course."

We left feeling pretty good. We just hoped that Mama would like it—but really, there was nothing to not like.

On the way home I called my landlord, Frankie, who lived next door, and asked him if he would help us bring Mama down the stairs. I also mentioned that a bottle of Wild Turkey would be his reward, and he said he would be delighted and to call when we got home. Susan, Janet, and I went upstairs and told Mama how much we liked the place and the owner.

"Well, will they take me? Will they be able to lift me?"

"They assured me that they could, but I want to make sure that you approve before we go any further."

"Okay, dear. Let's go."

It took Frankie and two of us to manage Mama in her wheelchair down fifteen steps, but we did it and it wasn't too bumpy a ride for her.

The driveway to Poppy Garden Villa was lined with Mexican sage in full purple bloom with dozens of hummingbirds feeding on the blossoms. Gorgeous California poppies were shining in the sunlight behind the sage. Mama used to paint California poppies so that meant a great deal to her.

The moment we arrived, Lilly romped out to greet us, along with two staff members. They introduced themselves to Mama while I struggled to get the wheelchair out of the trunk of the car. I wheeled the chair to the passenger side of the car where Mama was sitting. We stepped out of the way and the caregivers did their thing. They transferred her from the car to the wheelchair like pros, then wheeled Mama in and we met one of the residents, Mr. Holman, who was sitting in a chair watching an old Western on a large television set. He wasn't in bad shape. He walked and got around just fine. His problem was his memory loss, so he had a private caregiver 24/7. Besides his memory loss, Mr. Holman liked to go around with his willy hanging out, which was a problem for the neighbors on his walks. Mr. Holman was a die-hard cowboy. Always had been and always would be. His attire was a plaid western shirt, western cowboy boots, and a cowboy hat. He wore nothing but blue jeans and his skinny little legs were bowed from years of horseback riding. And he was a yodeler. He couldn't always remember that he knew how, but once you asked him to, he got serious and went into a classic cowboy lament of "Get Along Little Doggie." Mr. Holman's room was right across the hall from Mama's and was decorated with old black and white photographs of him roping on his horse.

Then there was Maria. She was a tiny little waif of a woman whose eyeglasses took up more than half her face. Maria had two martinis with olives every evening. Once I asked her if she wanted another martini and she replied, "Oh no dear, I am already feeling these. I don't want to get drunk." Maria never knew that her martini consisted only of Sprite and olives.

Mama liked her room. We sat on her bed and imagined where we would hang some of her paintings and the "damn branch." We opened the sheers, and quail scattered in all directions. It was sunny on her deck. We wheeled Mama all around the facility; then Julia came around the corner, went right up to Mama, and introduced herself.

"Hi Ellen, I'm Julia. What do you think of your room?"

Mama was smiling, "Oh, I think it's beautiful, dear, but can you handle me?"

Julia got right down in her face.

"If it's okay with you, I will come over to your house tomorrow and I will evaluate you. Is that alright?"

Mama was so cute. "That would be fine, dear. What time would you like to come?"

I laughed and asked Mama, "Why? Do you have to be somewhere tomorrow?"

She laughed, "No, I guess not. I'll see you tomorrow."

Since we had Mama out, we decided to wheel her around the neighborhood. It was a wonderful spot, and the homes and yards were beautifully maintained. The change of scene was great for her, and if she moved in, we could wheel her around all the time.

Julia showed up the next day, evaluated Mama, and announced to us that she would be very happy to accept her. Mama grinned, widened her eyes, and put both of her hands in the air and yelled, "Hooray!"

I walked Julia out and we spoke about the cost. It was $5,500 per month, and Mama would need to have a TB test. We decided on a date toward the end of the month to begin the process. Suddenly, I was overwhelmed and sad at what was happening. I knew Mama would miss Incha and Toes, but hopefully Lilly would make friends with her and take their place.

Top priority now was to get some potted flowers on the deck, along with her bird feeders and birdbaths. I put Susan on that. She was always eager to jump in, work hard, and schlep whatever had to be schlepped. She would show up with sandwiches and help until the work was complete. Susan is the most dependable person on earth.

Everything I did in the beginning, I had to do in reverse. Arrange to have the hospital bed moved, along with the lift chair. Take the shower chair and commode back to the Carmel Foundation. Explain her meds, write out their schedule, and have them transferred to another pharmacy. Call the doctor, make lists of what Mama liked and didn't like, let the caregivers go, arrange for her TB test, put money into a different account, and take care of stacks and stacks of paperwork.

It was happening. My prayers were answered and the miracle had manifested. My six months with Mama was over and I was feeling morose but hoped she would be happy at Poppy Garden Villa. The name was certainly appropriate, with her love of poppies. So back into production I went. We had a week.

When I climbed into bed that night, I lit a candle and remembered to thank the souls that helped from beyond to manifest this miracle: Dad, Jesus, Mama's best friend Harriet, her sister Connie, the Blessed Mother, Jimmy Durante, God, Louis Armstrong, Quan Yin, Bobby Darin, and Buddha. *Thank you all.*

CHAPTER 18

Mama's new home was enchanting, and her own paintings graced the walls. One of my favorites is an oil titled "Poppy Garden." It is a large square painting, with a background of an ethereal green fog that wraps itself around coral, pink, orange, and white poppies in different stages of their growth: budding with their little hairy heads face down, ready to bloom, full bloom, dying, and dead. The flowers in the mist are captivating because they are soft and mysterious. In the distance you just see a wisp of a wilting blue delphinium.

We placed Mama's angels all around the room, with her favorite one hung at the head of her bed. The angel's face, wings, feet, and hands were ceramic, and she wore a stiff taffeta peach-colored robe, with a pale yellow sash and a sky-blue shawl. Her wings were an ivory color with two shades of blue around the edges. She was about seven inches tall and had a sweet, angelic face. The paint was crude, but it enhanced the charm and spirit of this little blue-eyed beauty. Above the angel, looking a bit tired and sparse, and short two birds now, we once again secured the "damn branch."

We left Mama exhausted but peaceful, with a belly full of Clouds. She still had chocolate on her lips when I kissed her goodbye. I turned her lift chair so she could face outside. The birds were in their birdbath, singing, partying, and splashing water all over the deck. I opened one of the French doors and a consoling, balmy breeze embraced us as the sun began to set.

The staff brought her dinner and it looked scrumptious: fresh grilled salmon with lots of lemon, rice, asparagus, and homemade apple pie. It was time to let go and allow them to take over. I said good-bye with tears in my eyes, and hugged and kissed Mama. It was a struggle for me to give up control.

A main concern was that she would get her meds on time. I went over her med schedule again and again and bought a pill organizer. Julia assured me she would get up at 4:00 a.m. Mama was in their hands now.

I drove into my driveway and instinctively tried to remember which caregiver was there. Incha and Toes ran to me, relieved and happy because they panicked at the sight of suitcases heading out the door all day. Then I noticed a lot of leaves on the deck, a reminder that no caregiver had been around.

The silence in the house was deafening. No hello. No aroma of Glenda's cooking. No 40s music blasting from upstairs. I was alone. Since it was kitty cocktail hour, the cats and I went into the kitchen. I found my favorite cobalt blue glass, opened the freezer, filled it with ice, grabbed the vodka and set everything on the counter. There I spotted Mama's meal tray with the brightly-colored Guatemalan place mat, the little vase I used for her flowers, the neatly folded yellow napkin, her little salt and pepper shakers, and hardest of all, her sippy cup. Tears streamed down my face. *Oh God, did I do the right thing?*

All three of us sat on the couch. Then Incha started calling for Mama. Toes snuggled on my lap with paws outstretched as I did a toast to Mama. I took a sip, lit a candle and said a prayer that she would be happy.

I reflected on the last six months, and then in a flash, I realized I would have my bedroom back. I dragged the vacuum out of the closet and headed upstairs, tripping over the hose every third stair. I went into light speed: I scrubbed the bathroom, polished the floor, shined the mirrors, dusted the chests, and swept the upstairs deck, which was pretty empty now. Poor Norm was probably beside himself wondering what happened to his hummingbird feeder, so I made a note to get a new one for him the next day.

I went back downstairs and took my double bed apart, and piece-by-piece, dragged the frame, the box spring and the mattress up to my bedroom. I put a dust ruffle and clean sheets on, and then hauled up my nightstand and lamp.

Within thirty seconds after I flopped down on my freshly made bed, Toes and Incha joined me. The sun had set, but the sky glowed in all shades of blues, purples, oranges, pinks, and blood red. Darkness was setting in, and then one very bright, lone star popped out. I thought of a sympathy card someone had sent when Dad died. It said that stars are windows to heaven. I love that. If I had the most powerful telescope in the world, I could peek through a star and see Dad up there playing golf with Jesus, telling his same old jokes over and over as Jesus rolled his eyes. I missed Dad.

Just then, Norm's silhouette appeared at the window and I promised him I'd have that new feeder in the morning. And right on schedule, his mate beckoned him away for the last time that evening.

I missed Mama. I felt proud, honored, and privileged to have been her hero, but I felt more proud, honored and privileged to be her daughter. I am who I am because of her. She would have done this for me, and certainly with more grace. She was the hero. Mama gave a great gift to all of us. We lived a story that will touch people's hearts and spirits and help them realize that a day will come when their own Mama won't be there. You know that question you always meant to ask her, but thought you had forever to ask it? You don't. Regardless of how it seems at the moment, the truth is, she won't live forever.

I took a deep breath and remembered that for the first time in months, I didn't have to set the alarm. That part was over, but my love for Mama would never diminish. She was all about love. Unconditional. I am so lucky to have her for my Mama, and I will forever hold dearest to my heart that time we spent together.

EPILOGUE

We felt angels begin to descend around Thanksgiving. Mama spent more time sleeping and her speech had begun to slur.

By Christmas, she could barely keep her eyes open. When I fed her, she had difficulty chewing and swallowing. The osteoporosis had settled into her neck and now it affected her throat.

Mama's sleep patterns had changed too. Sometimes she lay awake late into the night, so the staff gave her Tylenol PM rather than a prescribed sleeping pill. At my suggestion, they stopped giving her the Tylenol PM, because now she drifted off to sleep in mid-sentence. I thought that her dozing off was perhaps the Tylenol working its way out of her system, but her pattern didn't change long after we stopped giving it to her.

Meanwhile, for months I'd been planning a trip to visit my friends Max and Gael who live in Tasmania. I met them when I was living in Bali in the 80s. They've visited here several times, but I never got a chance to visit them. I booked a flight with a nonrefundable, nontransferable, non-anything ticket. I was to leave January 24, the day after Mama's 90th birthday. I planned to be gone three weeks and spend my birthday in Tasmania with Max and Gael under a full moon. Then I'd head to Brisbane, Australia and hang out with my American friend, Lani, who worked for the university. By January though, the idea of leaving Mama was a huge concern. Susan and I discussed what I would do "if." I told her to call me if Mama spiraled downhill because it was essential for me to be with Mama when she died. If Mama just passed in her sleep while I was gone, then Susan was to call me, and I would make a decision at that time.

The second week in January, Mama could barely speak or swallow. I discussed this with Julia and called Dr. Hart and begged him to make a house call. He agreed to come see Mama. I phoned him on a Monday and called every day to make sure that he wouldn't forget. I wondered if she'd had a TIA, (ministroke) because of her slurring. Thursday I was able to spend some time with her even though she could barely communicate with me by that time. Mama and I were so connected that we didn't need words. She was aware that I was going to Tasmania, but I didn't talk about it because I didn't want to distress her.

A local television show interviewed me about caregiving and the six months that I had Mama with me. In spite of her eyesight going and her hearing diminishing, she loved watching the taped interview over and over. I had already started writing this book, so every time I visited her, she asked to hear another chapter. Her enthusiasm about the book brought such joy to me that I couldn't wait to write more just so I could share it with her. I encouraged her to add or delete anything, but she would just listen with her eyes closed and say, "Don't change a word, darling."

By now, she was able to respond with only her eyes and heart. I remember feeling a little sad because there were about fifteen quail on her deck, and even though her little potted garden was thriving, she couldn't see her patio anymore. I understood that we may have had our last conversation earlier, and I wished I had known that then. I left Mama after about two hours and drove home facing the unbearable reality that Mama was slipping away.

The next day, the doctor called and said that he had seen her early that morning and that she looked pretty good. He told me that she did not have a stroke, but he was concerned with her swallowing problem and that she would most likely have to go on a liquid diet. He would send a nurse out to do a test on her throat. He didn't mention her speech because he woke her up, and like me, she was no damn good in the mornings.

Saturday, there was a Sea of Cortez photo exhibition at the Pacific Grove Natural History Museum. Susan's husband, Chuck Baxter, was among a group of marine biologists who retraced Steinbeck's trip with Ed (Doc) Ricketts to the Sea of Cortez in 1940. They chartered a boat similar to the one in the original expedition, and compared the marine life then and now. Most of our friends were attending this celebration, but I knew in my heart I would decline.

I worked at the shop that Saturday and stopped by Mama's on my way home. I was overwhelmed with the presence of angels the moment I walked in the front door. I went into Mama's room, and their wings were open. The room glowed. Mama was sitting up in her bed. Her face lit up when she saw me. I gently took her hand, kissed her and said, "Mama, I think you are moving again, only this time you are moving in with the angels."

Her face lit up.

"You've grown your own wings now and it's time for you to leave this old body and fly away home."

She muttered something. No matter how hard I tried, I couldn't understand what her words were, but I knew what she was saying.

"Are you scared?" She shook her head and mumbled, "No."

I kissed her again and held onto her. We were looking beyond each other's eyes and into our souls. I couldn't hold back my tears.

"Mama, I love you so much. You have been the most perfect Mama in the entire world. Release yourself from this planet. You don't deserve the suffering and pain. No more. Let it all go now. Fly." Our eyes were locked.

"Maybe when you get to the other side you can do a little channeling after you settle in up there and help me finish the book." I could tell she was proud of me.

"I am who I am because of you, you know?" We laughed a little and her smiled broadened.

I held her a little longer and told her I was heading home but that I would be back in the morning and spend the whole day with her and spend the night.

"Good-bye, Mama, I will see you in the morning. I know you will sleep with the angels tonight because I can feel them. I love you." I couldn't tell her enough times.

She slurred, "I love you, too, darling." Those were the last words I heard my Mama speak.

I had invited a friend over for dinner so I had to head home. That was the hardest drive— ever. I wanted to turn the car around and be with Mama. I could barely see the road through my tears. I still regret that I didn't stay with her.

The next morning, Susan and I decided to head to Mama's early. I brought my sleeping bag as I still planned to sleep over. I knew Mama was coming to the end and I didn't want her to be alone. We arrived around 9:00 a.m. and much to our horror, Mama had slipped into an altered state of consciousness and I knew I would never hear her tell me that she loved me again. The night before, I had called Janet and she arrived around the same time we did. I also called my niece Christine and told her.

I rubbed some lavender oil on Mama's feet. A friend had told me that it helps the transition, and Mama did like to smell nice. I put on one of Mama's favorite CDs, songbirds from back east singing, accompanied by gentle music. Susan went out on the deck and watered the flowers, put more birdseed in the feeder and poured fresh water in the birdbath. I read more chapters to Mama that I had written. Whether she heard them or not, I'm not sure. Mama seemed to be struggling with the phlegm in the back of her throat. Shary happened to call me and ask if she and our close friend Susie could come over. I was glad to hear her voice and pleased that they were coming. I explained Mama's condition to Shary, and she suggested I call the doctor to see if he would send a hospice nurse over. I spoke with Dr. Hart's colleague and he agreed.

Minutes later, a hospice nurse called me. "I understand that your mother is DNR, (Do Not Resuscitate) is that right?"

"Yes." I answered quietly.

"Are you aware that this could be the end and are you prepared to face the reality?"

"Yes."

She told me that the struggling was not that horrible for Mama. It's worse for us to hear than it is for her. She said she would be there about 6:30.

Around 3:00, Shary and Susie arrived with a basket of goodies, including some wine. The dog, Lilly, trotted in to visit, sat at Shary's feet, then looked up at her aware that she was seeing a real angel. We kept the music going and the ambiance cheerful. Then Shary went out in the hall to greet and console her daughter, Jessica who had just arrived. I joined them and Jessica threw her arms around me crying and said, "Grandma is dying." I had been Jessica's nanny over 25 years before, and she was as close to Mama as any grandchild could be.

Shary suggested we tell stories about Mama.

I decided to go first. "OK, I've got one." And I began. "When I was in tenth grade, I was in a boarding school about an hour away from our home. Mama and Dad didn't want to send me there, but I insisted and begged, so they enrolled me. I was also a figure skater and a member of a precision group called the "Hockettes." It was quite prestigious and wonderful traveling in ice shows, wearing sparkly costumes, and meeting famous skaters. I loved being a Hockette and I didn't want to quit because of boarding school. Most of the boarders at St. Mary's Academy were required to go home for the weekends but needed to be back by Sunday night. My dilemma was that the Hockettes practiced on Sunday evenings, so Mama made special arrangements for me to return to school Monday mornings before classes began. Those mornings, Mama woke up in the dead of winter, before daylight. She went outside in the bone-chilling weather—sometimes even while it was still snowing—to scrape the ice and snow off the windshield and turn on the heat. Then she drove me an hour to school, dropped me off, and turned right around and drove home. That is unconditional love.

I went to her bedside, took her hand, kissed her, and thanked her.

Shortly after that, the hospice nurse, Gina, showed up ahead of schedule. This small, gentle, sensitive little being was so compassionate, yet professional and candid about what was happening. By now, Mama was getting dehydrated and her temperature was skyrocketing. Gina spoke softly, "I am ordering morphine for her pain and something that will relax her throat. Of course, by this time there was only one pharmacy open and it was about eight miles out of town. Shary and Susie didn't skip a beat and left to pick it up. I had been to that pharmacy on a Sunday evening and feared they would have a long, long wait.

Miracle of miracles, they were back within a half an hour. Gina administered the meds under Mama's tongue and showed Julia how to do it every fifteen minutes. We finished up some paperwork, then I sat on the floor in between Jessie's legs and we watched the change in Mama. Her face relaxed, they turned her on her side, and her breathing softened.

Jessie, touching my hair, said, "Grandma's going. She is slipping away."

I thought that Mama was just relaxing from the drugs. I got up to walk Gina out the door.

Jessie came out into the hall and quietly motioned to me.

"Bethie, come here."

I arrived at Mama's side just in time to touch her while she took her last breath, then I announced, "Mama is gone."

My sister, Janet, leaned over Mama and sobbed hysterically, and Susan also bent down to kiss Mama good-bye.

I looked up, and her radiant wings were spread and softly soaring accompanied by angels. It was a glorious moment for me and I laughed and cried at the same time.

I knew that I would never look into those blue eyes again or touch those soft hands or wipe chocolate off her mouth again. My whole being felt full of grace and light and joy. All of us present felt an indescribable bond. We call it the "Bubble of Grace."

Mama died at 8:40 p.m. on January 14, 2007. Forty-five minutes later, a weeping Julia took me aside and said, "We are going to have to call the mortuary some time tonight, but there is no hurry."

Only one immediate thought popped into my head, and maybe it was from Mama. "Call them now. I feel no attachment to this body that caused her so much agony. She flew out of that prison. Mama isn't in there anymore. It's just a shell."

Kathleen made the call and within forty minutes, they were there.

Two days later I discovered that mortuaries are like vultures. They prey on your loss. They charged us an exorbitant amount of money just for a cardboard box to transport her from the mortuary to the crematorium. We looked at some of the urns for her, and the only container that was even remotely acceptable was a cardboard heart-shaped box made of rice paper with little rosebuds in it. I have seen them at the craft stores for around $5.00. They wanted $359 for it. People are so full of grief and don't want to look cheap, so they go for unreasonably priced items, whether it is a casket or an urn. Even the death certificate cost was outrageous. Mama would rather we spend the money on a fun dinner out. Then I remembered a sweet pink floral box that I had bought for her not long before. She loved it and kept her scarves in it. It would suit her just fine.

The mortician asked us if we wanted to put anything in with her. Susan and I looked at each other and I said, "the damn branch." We took all the birds off except three, representing her three daughters. We included the angel that hung on the wall above her head, and we couldn't let Mama pass to the afterlife without a Cloud.

That night, I sat on my bed with Toes and Incha writing this book. The drapes were closed and it was just after sunset. It occurred to me that Mama's leaving meant that I was free to get on the plane to Tasmania with no worries about her. What an incredible gift she bestowed on me by choosing to pass when she did. I opened up the curtains and expected to see a star so bright that it was unmistakably Mama saying that she was happy, pain-free and shining. But to my surprise, there was not one star in the cloudy sky that night. All I could do was throw my head back and laugh and say, "Well, good for you, Mama, you're probably off having a glass of champagne with Rembrandt or Renoir, Dad, E.J. and all your friends. Enjoy this time and don't worry about us. I know you will forever love me and forever be with me. I feel such joy for you. Good night Mama. I love you. Fly with the angels.

Obituaries

Ellen E. Harris
January 23, 1917 ~ January 14, 2007

"Poppy Garden"

"I am not a
dispassionate painter
and am not interested
in rendering.
My longing is to
depict the exquisiteness
in the line of a stem,
a small pool of pure color,
the elusive grace of a
dying flower, or the light
nearly erasing the vision.
I am still trying."